SPIRITUAL SIDE OF SEX

SPIRITUAL SIDE OF SEX

THE DANGEROUS PATH OF AN UNSENSORED SEX LIFE

DR. EVETTE YOUNG

GOD'S ROYAL WOMEN

This book and all other God's Royal Women™ books are available at Christian bookstores and distributors worldwide. To order products, or for any other correspondence:

GOD'S ROYAL WOMEN™ USA

 Email: media@godsroyalwomen.org

Or reach us on the Internet: www.godsroyalwomen.org

ISBN 13: 978-1-0879-1056-7

For Worldwide Distribution, Printed in the U.S.A.

Disclaimer

Dr. Evette Young is a doctor of Theology and a Minister of the Gospel of Jesus Christ. In this capacity, I provide information related to spiritual matters. We do not provide services as medical professionals or give advice based on medical diagnosis. Any advice which are given in this material, is based upon the Holy Bible and personal experiences, and is meant for the purposes of bringing individuals into a closer relationship with God, the Father, and with His Son, Jesus Christ. Dr. Evette has many years of experience in the Ministry and believe that most problems are spiritual in nature.

We are not responsible for individuals who read this material and act upon it to the detriment or injury of themselves or others. We are not diagnosticians or psychiatrists. When we refer to a psychological or physical symptom, we are giving information which will guide you in gaining deliverance, not a medical treatment. If you are being treated by a physician or psychologist, we do not recommend that you stop any treatments until a physician recommends you do so.

Dedication

This book is dedicated God the Father, Son and the Holy Spirit.

Acknowledgments

Special thanks to:

My husband Apostle (Dr.) John King Hill and my precious daughter Anointed Evelyn-Divine, for all your support and encouragements.

My Father and mother: Mr. & Mrs. Emmanuel and Evelyn Young for their many years of hard work and supporting me!

Dr. D. K. Olukoya, Mountain of Fire, Nigeria, West Africa.

Pastor Rod Parsley, World Harvest Church, Columbus, Ohio.

Bishop R.C. & Lisa Blake, New Home Fellowship, USA.

Apostle Victor Ronnie Nnamdi, Nigeria, West Africa.

Prophet Samuel & Eunice Addison, Eagles House Chapel In-ternational, Ghana, West Africa.

Contents

Introduction

Sex as a created work has a spiritual and physical purpose, but the way sexual act is used in societies can lead to misappropriation. Lack of understanding about sex has caused major problems in the lives of many people everywhere. Anything that pertains to life requires extraordinary depth to uncover the secrets. Life as a mystery offers beyond what no learned behaviors can substitute for. Because living life involves experimenting, exercising sexual right — to engage in sexual activities can open a person's life to spiritual and physical complications.

Spiritual Side of Sex has carefully addressed the complexities of different sexual behaviors to expose the hidden dangers. Often, people do not understand the separation of rights versus rule of law and order of life. They trespass and expand beyond their zone of freedom. Freedom is as thin as air and water, so people pierce themselves through hard bondage out of ignorance spiritually and physically. If your right takes you into bondage, you have sacrificed important part of your life.

Sex has restrictions that govern the boundaries to limit sexual irregularities. This is because sex was created from governmental structured environment; therefore, the use must fall within proper jurisdictions. People think that their bodies are their personal properties and they can do whatever they want. They can give their bodies sexually to anyone they feel an attraction and affection for. They underestimate the consequences of violating the rule of sex. The danger is that sexual consent is part of a person's willful decision to engage in a sexual act. The bigger problem is the condition that is set forth to engage in a sexual contact.

Fornication and adultery are not love and likewise, inordinate affections and attractions that break the barriers of sexual confinement are not love. Lust and perversion are like learning to swim in the middle of the ocean. Venturing into the eternal realm without spiritual guidance is risking your life forever. One decision in life is enough to cost you everything. There is no way that the human race will understand sex without knowing the life of God to limit the misuse. The character that enhances and over-qualifies life to endure eternally takes more than human establishment. Wrongful acts are equivalent to personal betrayal so many people will destroy their own lives by just one simple act.

Our rights can never supersede God's sovereignty over our lives. The keys of our lives are hidden from us. Therefore, reasonable answers do not carry the weight legal judgment. Sex can be weaponized as sex can be commercialized: the exchange of sex whether for service or vengeful warfare are misappropriation and the consequences are never overlooked. Spiritual Side of Sex has laid great emphasis on the blind-spots that sexual fantasies and sexual ecstasy does not reveal during sexual intercourse. People sex their lives to destruction today because of sexual feeling! Man and woman are not sex machines: image after the likeness of God goes beyond a toy factory and humans are not figurines. They are given life with great responsibilities even when they are totally unaware or lack the true knowledge of who they are.

I have personally gone over the entire contents of Spiritual Side of Sex and found compelling hidden truth about sexuality and the consequences of violating the original rules of the Creator. Sex organs are not to be played with, and those who are managers of these organs must know that playing with fire and gas is risking one hundred percent burn. Some warfare cannot be won because everything in life is not just a fight. This is why underlying truth is the key to the wholeness of the people of God. Ye shall know the truth and the truth will make you free! As you read this material, please pray that the LORD God will catapult your deliverance from soul-ties, sex-ties and demonic ties! May the LORD save you from sexual addiction, lust, perversion and all inordinate cravings.

In His Love,

Apostle (Dr.) John King Hill,

Author, Men of Purpose

www.johnkinghillministries.com

Preface

Over the years, I have gone through many difficult challenges — seeking for personal deliverance. Each stop I made provoked my curiosity to search for the true reason why many people are not free. Why are men and women of God saying things that people are not realizing in their conditions or situations. I come to understand that unless you have gone through a lonely road, embarked upon a deliverance journey and stood on every healing line without seeing your breakthrough, you may never understand the discouragement of people everywhere today. You would take them lightly or see them strange in some way.

The fight for real freedom is not for those who lack spiritual and physical stability: the pressure is like climbing a mountaintop. The air suddenly dries up and the thirst and hunger to see the end evaporates — leaving only a mist of fog. Sometimes we capture the mirage of life, hoping to turn the mirror image into living realities. The compartments of life have many clues to resolving the issues of life; however, deep problems call for deep exploration and until we discover the prescription, we cannot prescribe cures. A quack doctor cannot be separated from a fool!

Spiritual Side of Sex has been written to show the intricate secrets of sexuality and why sex is more than male and female genders could really explain. The mysteries of sex takes more than what we feel — the drive and passion for sexual contact. The implications of Irresponsible sexual behaviors can open the floodgates of consequential repercussions that the impacts will last for years or even generations. In the old days, sex was not a common dialogue among different cultures: it was something secretive even though people were engaging in sexual intercourse. We are in a more open society today and the sex crave is explicitly open to the public.

Sexual open doors and luring temptations are no longer hidden. Sex trades exist even as sexual molestation and abuses are prevalent. Societies are bombarded by sexual contents — making it easier to embrace pornography and masturbation besides other hardcore sexual behaviors. The pull to continue to explore different sexual experimentation have driven many people into the pits of sexual abyss. Sexuality today has become more commercialized among us and children are being swept up into sexual victimization. The safeguards that make sex sacred has been destroyed through lust and perversion. Families are wrecked and the disability has left trails of wounded and destroyed victims of sexual molestation and abuses.

Households have wrap sheets of sex offenders hiding under the covers of family secret books. This is why bondage run deep in many families because deliverance does not come without true repentance. Hiding the family secrets are not the key to addressing bloodline curses; therefore, we are seeing common trends among family groups everywhere. As I speak to men and women around the world today, they share similar testimonies without knowing each other personally. What is happening in one place is also being experienced in different other places. What breaks my heart is their destitution and desperation to be set free. Many of them have been to several places — seeking for help.

The wounds of rape, incest and other sexual molestation can leave people with traumatic memories for a lifetime. Many lives are damaged today because of one or two sexual encounters. The misuse of sex in the societies has created webs of damaging pain and hurt, and the victims are desperately hopeless and helpless. This book has been carefully designed to enlighten and to bring dramatic solution and cure for your sexual suffering. I want to help you break free. I want to see you receive your deliverance both spiritually and physically. I want to watch your life shift and I want to hear your personal testimony about God's saving, healing and deliverance power in your life.

In His Service,

Prophetess (Dr.) Evette Young

Chapter One

SEX IN OUR SOCIETIES

In today's sex inundated world, everywhere you turn the media is spreading advertisements based on sex. We see so many impressions and expressions, alluring eyes and minds to captivate their audiences. It's very hard for many people to remain innocent because of the constant bombardment. In the context of spiritual side of sex, I will attempt to enlighten you on the deeper spiritual side, not just the physiological side of sex. I believe there is a great deal of ignorance concerning the mysteries of sexual intercourse. Sex is not talked about much or lectured on in our religious settings today, even though the Bible has much to say on the subject of sex. We know that people are having sex outside of marriage because there are many countless single mothers and abortions all over the places. We know that many people have been sexually molested and raped, but the Church tends to shy away from this issue.

Sex is something designed by the Creator for one man and one woman as husband and wife (See Genesis 2:21-

24). We see from the biblical account that sex is to be reserved within the confines of marriage, and marriage is to be the only outlet for expressing our sexual needs.

1 Corinthians 7:2-5 states, *but because of the temptation to impurity and to avoid immorality, let each [man] have his own wife and let each [woman] have her own husband. The husband should give to his wife her conjugal rights (goodwill, kindness, and what is due her as his wife), and likewise the wife to her husband. For the wife does not have [exclusive] authority and control over her own body, but the husband [has his rights]; likewise, also the husband does not have [exclusive] authority and control over his body, but the wife [has her rights]. Do not refuse and deprive and defraud each other [of your due marital rights], except perhaps by mutual consent for a time, so that you may devote yourselves unhindered to prayer. But afterwards resume marital relations, lest Satan tempt you [to sin] through your lack of restraint of sexual desire.*

1 Corinthians 6:18 says, *shun immortality and all sexual looseness (flee from impurity in thought, word, or deed). Any other sin which a man commits is one outside the body, but he who commits sexual immorality sins against his own body.*

We can see from the above Scriptures that sex has mysterious connotations. We must look into why sex outside of marriage causes one to sin against his own body, and what are the consequential ramifications. We live in a sexually steeped and saturated generation — a generation that is submerged and intoxicated with sex. We are seeing increased lust and perversion like no other time in history. Sex is satan's number one weapon, that he continues to use against this pleasure-seeking generation. Sex is spiritual and a serious act of exchanging energies and power, and we should not treat it like kids playing with loaded machine guns.

We see how satan plays on the minds of the people, and the mind is one of the battlefields of all temptation. Satan uses sexual temptation to entice people. He wants people to see only the good side of sexual feeling and the pleasurable satisfaction or fulfillment of sex! He never reveals what the awful aftermath of the initial elation and climax would expose their lives to. There are those who consume sexual sin like drinking water or the air they breathe. It may feel pleasurable; however, you will discover later that it is drinking from polluted water. I want to encourage you to please stay on and keep reading!

In Matthew 15:19 the Bible says, *for out of the heart comes evil thoughts reasoning and disputing and designs such as murder adultery, sexual vice, theft, false witness, slander and irrelevant speech.*

Mark 7:21 recorded, *for from within that is out of the hearts of men, come base and wicked thoughts, sexual immorality, stealing, murder, adultery. But I say to you that everyone who so much as looks at a woman with evil desire (lust) for her has already committed adultery with her in his heart.*

Today, the living word of God is no longer the standard upon which we define our sexual values. Our society is in a sex crisis. Sexual proclivities and other issues are at the root of many addictions and bondage across our cultures. 85-95 % of marriages that ended in divorce was rooted in pre-marital sex. Not having sex outside of marriage does not guarantee a happy marriage; however, illegal sex will cause a tremendous amount of long-term damage. When God created our bodies, it was not created for abuse or for our sexuality to be broken or vandalized through immorality. God created us with a healthy sexuality in mind.

Many of us including myself grew up in homes, where the first sexual encounter was a forceful interference -- violations from family members, which opened our lives to incest implications. And because of such hideous acts, many people are scared and some have developed pathological lifestyles. Incest is any form of sexual conduct whether oral, anal, or genital penetration between bloodline relatives. Sexual abuse by foster care parents and step-parents are also considered as incest. What we have to remember is that incest is a silent epidemic; it damages the character structures of the victims with serious long-term consequences. It leads to all sorts of confusion: identity, marriage, friendship, parental relationships, families and society, etc.

We must have interventions and systems in place to help those who were harmed through incest violations. The reason is that incest, family breakdowns, and sexual distortions are closely related. From a spiritual perspective, incest is a major opening for demonic spirits to attach themselves to the victims. It's a great open door, which means that it sets the stage for spiritual implications down the road. The truth of the matter is, our society is in a crisis. Many people are sexually damaged and their lives are affecting others like plaques or viruses. Sexual abuse and molestation are at an all-time high. The average American will see 15,000 sexual references a year on television alone. Pornography brings in over $39 billion. 45 percent of clergy have admitted to struggling with pornography. We must admit today that something is severely wrong. We must begin to implement safe avenues to help our societies from this infiltration and pandemic.

As a matter of fact, the first person that took your virginity was the first to create a blood covenant with you. The covenant was formed when the hymen was broken and blood was produced and the blood pressure from the male's erection coming together. The consummation through intercourse immediately created a very powerful covenant between the two parties involved. Covenants are more powerful than contracts! Therefore, it is why sex is not only a physical contact, but a spiritual connection. The energies of each person interconnects as well as the DNA – linking or intertwining the fluids and secretions. This bonding can take several years to dissolve. Scientifically, it has been researched that spermatozoa do not die inside of the female's body but swims to different parts of the body and stays there forever to become a living part of your DNA. Sperm is alive. They are living cells. I encourage you to do your own research on male micro-chimerism, living in a female's body, you would be amazed at what you will discover.

1 Corinthians 6:15-16 says, *know ye not that your bodies are the members of Christ? Shall I then take the members of Christ, and make them the members of a harlot? God forbids. What? Know ye not that he which is joined to a harlot is one body? For two, saith he, shall be one flesh.*

Sex is a mystery, but what I have also discovered is that it is not something anyone should enter into carelessly and casually. Knowledge eliminates mystery in life and also when applied, it helps to bring an end to needless suffering and pain. Let us not remain in ignorance concerning spiritual matters.

For the LORD thy God walketh in the midst of thy camp, to deliver thee, and to give up thine enemies before thee; therefore shall thy camp be holy: that he see no unclean thing in thee, and turn away from thee (Deuteronomy 23:14).

Chapter Two

SEXUALLY TRANSMITTED DEMONS

It is hereby evident that, because the wages of sin are death when you sin against your own body, you incur spiritual and physical damages. Your body will be negatively impacted with spiritual and physical implications and complications. Spirits of death will have a legal right to attack you by bringing disease elements inside of your body and soul. What we clinically know to be sexually transmitted diseases are in the spirit sexually transmitted demons. Demons bring with them their nature and assignment to carry out on a person's life each time there is an occasion to exploit his or her life through sinful behaviors.

This subject has been neglected in many religious settings for so long, even though people are experiencing such strange occurrences. In Genesis 6:2-4, the Bible said, *the sons of God saw the beautiful women and took them as their wives*. Evil spiritual marriage is real. In those days, and sometime thereafter, the Nephilim lived on the earth. Nephilim or giants are not merely in times of the structural looks but spiritual, so there are different theological beliefs and doctrinal concepts about the Nephilim. When the "sons of God" whether this terminology fits our belief or not, had sexual intercourse with women, they gave birth to generic – or hybrid offspring, who became heroes and famous warriors of ancient times. Even though we do not see giants walking the earth today, the spirits of those giants never left the earth realm; in fact, they have been tormenting lives ever since then. This is why you may see a giant having sex with you in dreams, or you see yourself giving birth to creatures in your dreams. You may see yourself breast-feeding in a dream, swimming in a river, bathing a baby in a dream. These dreams are strong indicators that you might be experiencing spiritual attacks by evil spirits who are claiming you as their spouse(s). The babies that many of you see in dreams are spiritual offspring from spiritual spouse(s).

The spiritual realm is a deep realm. Many people are encountering these phenomena and the truth is that you are not crazy or hallucinating, as some unfamiliar people may assume or presume. What you are dealing with, from a spiritual perspective, is very real. If you share your experience with certain individuals, some will not believe you because they have no point of reference in their own lives. They will doubt your account. However, this problem is widely spread, and many people are looking for real solutions today. Deep problems will always call for deep prayers and deep prayers come with deep spiritual insight. These issues will need the help of the LORD Jesus Christ to be fully delivered. You must know that you are dealing with a "this kind" of captivity and bondage. (See Matthew 17:21).

I must tell you that you do not have to remain in bondage; it is possible to be completely free! The Bible said, if the Son therefore shall make you free, ye shall be free indeed (John 8:36). We have to exercise diligent caution to see that lust and perversion can take us into very dangerous and deadly places of great torment. Lust is defined as an insatiable desire, intense or unbridled sexual desire, craving, and yearning for sexual climax. Anytime you get to a place where you can no longer control your sexual interest, you are in serious danger. The same applies to any time you trespass beyond the boundaries of normal (legal) sexual contacts and behaviors.

Many people today are being attacked by incubus and succubus, foul demons that haunt men and women all over the world. Incubus is defined as an evil spirit that lies on persons in their sleep: they oppress or burden like a nightmare. Succubus is a demon spirit assuming female form to have sexual intercourse with men in their sleep.

These horrible creatures constantly bombard your mind with sexually deviant thoughts and ideas until you begin to act upon the thoughts. They also are responsible for what is known as "wet dreams." These destructive spirits also are responsible for making you feel ashamed after your lust and pervasive behaviors have been conceived and acted upon. Their sole purpose is to live out their own sexual perversions through you! Their desire is to trap your soul and cause you to live a life of bondage, regret and torment. These demons can show up as serpents, dogs, or pigs in your dreams. They can transform and shape-shift into different looks and appearances. They can also take the faces of family members or loved ones as ways to disguise themselves and try to get you comfortable -- to relax yourself with them. They can appear as a girlfriend or boyfriend, a husband or wife, etc. A spirit husband and wife, boyfriend or girlfriend will also drive people into all sorts of uncontrollable sexual activities including but not limited to pornography and masturbation, whether privately or in public. These evil spirits are spirits of death and they often pressure their victims with suicidal thoughts to drive them to commit suicide.

This is why it is extremely important to live a clean and pure life, in your mind and your body. The realm of fantasy also opens people up to astral attacks. These are astral projected souls that you connect with in the astral plane. They can sodomize you and open your life up to be constantly bombarded by homosexual or lesbian thoughts, even though you never desired such inordinate affection and attraction. Many people are experiencing sleep paralysis or being held down and not able to call the name of Jesus even though they are using all of their strength to call out for help. These spirits zap your energy, rape you, and deposit all sorts of evil into your energy field. These are demonic energies! Evil spirits are tormenting billions of people across the world today.

Some people do not understand that fornication is sexual intercourse between two people who are not married. Even if you are not having penetration, oral sex and anal sex opens your life up to experience these hellish encounters with spirit husbands and wives or spirit boyfriends and girlfriends. Sex is spiritual and sex is food for idols. Sex is part of spiritual offering and sacrifices on the altars of pagan worship. Paul said their sacrifices are unto devils. (See 1 Corinthians 10:20).

The Bible says in Galatians 6:7-8, *be not deceived; God is not mocked: for whatsoever a man soweth, that shall he also reap. For he that soweth to his flesh shall of the flesh reap corruption; but he that soweth to the Spirit shall of the Spirit reap corruption; but he that sows to the Spirit shall of the Spirit reap life everlasting.*

Simply put, we must control our sex drives and guard our sexual behaviors. Sexual intercourse was to be enjoyed in its fullness in a proper marriage relationship.

Each time you come together in sexual intimacy, you are joining yourself together as one – spirit, soul and body, and you are connecting with demonic spirits. I want us to understand how extremely dangerous it is to have multiple sexual partners. Sex is a form of worship and sex was not only designed for procreation but for pleasure in its proper context. Each time a person engages in illegal sexual activity, he or she is forming a pact with demonic spirits. Devils are involved in all forms of sin, trespass, iniquity, transgression, and they actively encourage proclivities and unclean behaviors in people's lives. Demons look at sin as worship of satan! This is how the souls of many people get entangled and enslaved.

SPIRIT HUSBAND, WIFE, BOYFRIEND AND GIRLFRIEND: Spirit husband and wife or spirit boyfriend and girlfriend are demons impersonating the humans by exemplifying similar characteristics of either husband, wife, boyfriend and girlfriend. They play the roles of either genders, which is perversion besides fueling the passion of sexual lust. The relationship and roles of husband and wife are more established or permanent rather than a boyfriend and girlfriend. Therefore, the familiar spirits using lost and perversion must endeavor to gain entrance into the sexual organs of their victims to stimulate their sexual drives. Following and observing the individual to gather intelligence is not enough until they have access into the people's lives to influence or control their sexual desires and behaviors.

Spirits are immaterial, which is to say that they are not visible at all times although in the spirit realms, you can see their forms and hear them speak and interact. You may not see a spirit husband, wife, boyfriend, and girlfriend with the natural eyes, but spiritually you can interact with these spirits: in dreams, visions, and other activities. They are different from spirit guides because of their roles to connect with people sexually. People can be coerced to share intercourse spiritually or forcefully raped in the spirit realms, especially when the victim is held in sexual bondage. A sex slave does not have the honor of a respectable relationship, so he or she can be penetrated forcefully without first securing the consent for sexual intercourse.

Although the marriage bed must not be defiled: both married and unmarried people can be exposed to spirit husband, wife, boyfriend, and girlfriend in the spirit realms. The spirit husband will act as a husband! The spirit wife will act as a wife. The spirit boyfriend will act as a boyfriend and the spirit girlfriend will act as a girlfriend. All these delicate works are geared towards securing sexual contact with the victim to pollute and bring defilement in their lives. Remember, there is no gender in the spirit so the same demon may assume different forms including the resemblance of family members or loved ones, friends and associates, and even strangers, etc. The level of close-ness will show the kind of relationship whether a husband and wife or boyfriend and girlfriend relationship. For an example, husband and wife share the same house and everything while boyfriends and girlfriends may visit each other sometimes and engage in sexual contact. Some people will experience constant or periodic sexual contacts in the spirit.

HAVING SEX IN THE DREAMS: having sexual intercourse in the spirit may involve spirit husband, wife, boyfriend and girlfriend; however, it is not to say that a man and woman cannot dream about each other. Nevertheless, to be extremely careful, we must filter everything through the word of God, prayer and the Spirit of God. Therefore, we need the gift of discernment of spirits, the inspiration of the Spirit and the revelation of God. We must exercise caution to understand that demons taking the forms of either husband and wife represents a decision to hide their own identities. The spirit realms know that husband and wife are to share sexual intimacy. The spirit realms also know that boyfriend and girlfriend sexual contacts are violations of spiritual and physical orders of life. This is to say that a husband and wife can see each other sexually from spiritual perspective: sex is beyond the natural contact! Please do not forget that spiritual eyes can see beyond the fabrics of the physical materials! To fulfill all righteousness, it is highly important to seek deliverance evaluation as a precaution measure.

THE IMPLICATIONS: the works of spirit husband and wife are to interfere with the normal order of legitimate marriages. The spirits can affect the physical marriage from functioning in its full capacity and also prevent people from getting married. They can deprive the sexual life of a marriage by doing everything possible to hinder and deny sex in the marriage. In fact, spirit husband and wife are major causes of separation and divorce in marriages. Other factors are used only as tools of distraction and confusion.

LOSS OF ATTRACTION AND AFFECTION: spirit husband and wife can steal attraction and affection from marriages. One person can lose attraction and affection for the partner and the spirit husband and wife can instigate hatred among the two. This is why "they two must become one flesh" or inseparable from physical standpoint, but it is a matter of spiritual pillar or foundation! Spirit husband and wife can drive people into pornography and masturbation or open people into inordinate affection and attraction toward the opposite sex. Besides impacting people's genders to turn or pervert their sex appeals, they can drive people into prostitution and other forms of sexual immorality. Sexual immorality is part of the works of spirit husband and wife because the marriage bed must not to be defiled! In the world, boyfriend and girlfriend and other kinds of illicit relationships are promoted as alternative to lawful godly marriage. These relations flame the fires of lust and perversion to create a revolving door of sexual immoralities in the societies.

SEXUAL IMMORALITY: many husbands and wives are in sexual immoralities because of the works of a spirit husband and wife. Spirit husband and wife promote and divert the attraction and affections of husband and wife to involve others: men, women, and spirits in their marriages. Both the husband and wife are attracted to others but not to each other. Spirit husband can steal the attraction and affection of the husband from the wife, and spirit wife can steal the attraction and affection of the wife from the husband. The endgame is to change and transform the image of the man and woman: the genders are not only impacted, but who they are in God and what they represent. Demons manifest their images and reveal who they are or their nature in people! They do not want the image of Christ and God after His likeness! You must understand that the mark and image of satan morphs into his nature, which is the consummation of his likeness!

STOPPING PEOPLE FROM MARRYING: many people across the world – men and women are not married because of the works of spirit husband, wife, boyfriend and girlfriend. Spirit husband confronts men who try to engage with women who are under their powers, and the same applies to the spirit wife. They attack and torment people as ways to hinder them from legitimate marriages while driving their lives into lust and perversion. This is the way they achieve their satanic kingdom goals. Some people are in marriages but spirit husband and wife have made the relationship hard to consummate or flourish. The marriage is hostile and in constant tumult: there are no intimacy and no room to cultivate normalcy and order. If you are married and there is no attraction and affection, deprived of sexual intimacy, constantly in strange arguments and battles, there are spiritual elements: spirit husband, wife, boyfriend, or girlfriend contending against your marriage through marital counter-claims or accusations of infidelity. Having sexual contact with you in the spirit is the way to establish a case of defiling your marital bed. Many marriages have been separated and divorced because of the works of spirit husband, wife, boyfriend, and girlfriend. Spirit spouses, boyfriends, and girlfriends express jealous anger and rage. Although they may expose you to multiple men and women for sexual immorality, they will attempt to deny or stop you from committing to a legitimate marriage. They can attach to and torment whoever enters into marriage relationship with you to bring separation and divorce. Other characteristics of spirit husband and wife is sowing deception in the marriage that the woman is not good for the husband or the reverse. They can sow the seed of pride and stubbornness

SPIRITUAL SIDE OF SEX

to destroy the lives of the husband and wife beyond the marriage relationship unless they are delivered.

INABILITY TO CONCEIVE: sometimes, we hear about low sperm count or bareness – spirit husband and wife may attack the womb and block the tubes. They can cause miscarriages, hemorrhages, abortions, and sicknesses and diseases, etc. They defile the body to create open doors to access – gain entrance into people's body parts and cause them pain and failure. They can affect the sperm count or cause the sperm to deplete to zero. Some women can dream about being pregnant in the spirit, giving birth and breastfeeding but in true reality, they are unable to conceive. When demons engage in sexual intercourse with people, they are not only defiling but stealing, killing, and destroying – exchanging who you are and what you have for what they are offering or represent in the demonic Kingdom.

SICKNESSES AND DISEASES: spirit spouses infect people with sicknesses and diseases! Demons are not only infectious because they are unclean, they are symptomatic. Their presence is incompatible with the human body or makeup: they are not built to dwell inside of people. Angels are created for duty and not for relationship; therefore, they are forces. Fallen angels or demons are destabilization forces, so deformity, failure and other misfortunes are parts of abusive control to limit people from their full potential and functionality. They have strong will to achieve their assignments and often, it leads to excessive use of force, which is part of lust and perversion!

REVERSAL OF GENDERS: The Bible said, *So God created man in his own image, in the image of God created he him; male and female created he them* (Genesis 1:27). The designed roles and characteristics of both man and woman are clearly established from a spiritual perspective or order of life. A man is not a woman and a woman is not a man: this is a spiritual order. Therefore, genders are not the issues of mistaken identity! Even God, is a spirit and man, is flesh and blood! The great part of lust and perversion is to advance the knowledge of evil. Satan wants to exploit the order of human genders – to confuse or turn the woman to man or man to woman! Some order of living has been affected by this reversion: a woman is gentle, caring, submissive, helper, child care-giver or one who nurtures and raises her child, etc. A woman is not a built to fight against her house, disrespect her house, wreck her home and be careless for her children and quarrelsome. When a woman focuses all her affection on career, job, employment, equality and feminism, it can lead to reversed order and the impact on family will be greatly devastating.

Equality is never a comparison of both genders! It is never a competition among the genders or reversing the places and roles according to divine orders! It is never a contest between husband and wife. In society today, satanic agendas are clearly seen in our pursuits for careers, jobs, employments, money, wealth and riches over marriage, children, and family. There are those whom satan has turned from men to women and women to men even though they may be physically in the men or women's body. In married households, satan wants to reverse the roles of husbands and wives: the men become the women and the women become the men. This is a spiritual attack on the genders! It's completely demonic and a huge access door for sex demons to control one's destiny and ultimately steal, kill and destroy his or her life. Always keep in mind that satan is a thief, a killer and destroyer, and if you agree with his lies, he will impact your life. We must pray for households today because many people are suffering behind closed doors under demonic powers!

The Bibles recorded, *For even their women exchanged the natural use for what is against nature, likewise also the men, leaving the natural use of the woman, burned in their lust for one another, men with men committing what is shameful, and receiving in themselves the penalty of their error which was due* (Romans 1:26b & 27).

LOVE AND RESPECT: having spirit husband and wife can lead to dishonor and disrespect for your spouse physically. You cannot serve two masters! Spirit husband and wife make their spouses seem useless. They destroy the order of love and submission to cause power-struggle, hostility, and disloyalty. They create rivalry to undermine the common goals of the marriage relationship. Spirit husband and wife instigate authoritative and controlling behaviors. There is no abuse without manipulative control! These are the common signs of demonic powers wreaking havoc in marriages through slandering, speaking against one another, lying and deceiving, abusing, creating quarrels, arguments and fighting to make the marriage unstable. They strip spiritual and physical values from marriages to undercut the growth and maturity – prosperity! Husbands and wives must be careful not to bring their private lives into the mainstream and expose themselves! The events of the garden of Eden are still playing out in marriages today across the world in different cultures because of the cunning craftiness of the enemy.

And the man said, the woman whom thou gavest to be with me, she gave me of the tree, and I did eat. And the Lord God said unto the woman, what is this that thou hast done? And the woman said, the serpent beguiled me, and I did eat (Genesis 3:12-13).

THE POWER OF THE GOSPEL: *For I am not ashamed of the gospel of Christ: for it is the power of God unto salvation to everyone that believeth; to the Jew first, and also to the Greek* (Romans 1:16). The power of the gospel is the key to spiritual freedom whether it relates to demonic issues, poverty and lack, or sicknesses and diseases. There is a reason why true servants of Jesus Christ suffer persecution and some endure great tribulation: the authority of the name of Jesus Christ in and the power of the Holy Spirit are used against the satanic Kingdom. Deliverance or the ministry of casting out devils is attacking the demonic roots in the lives the lives of the people. It is undermining and eradicating the works of evil spirits and dismantling the Kingdom of satan inside of people to set them free. (See 1 John 3:8).

And these signs shall follow them that believe; In my name shall they cast out devils; they shall speak with new tongues; They shall take up serpents; and if they drink any deadly thing, it shall not hurt them; they shall lay hands on the sick, and they shall recover (Mark 16:17-18).

The Spirit of the Lord is upon me, because he hath anointed me to preach the gospel to the poor; he hath sent me to heal the brokenhearted, to preach deliverance to the captives, and recovering of sight to the blind, to set at liberty them that are bruised, To preach the acceptable year of the Lord (Luke 4:18-19).

Satan and his demons have no problems with those who profess to be Christians – or anyone preaching and teaching without the authority of Jesus Christ and the power of the Holy Spirit. The Holy Spirit is the secret of the true Christian life or the potency of the power of the gospel will be limited to mere rituals. Destroying the works of the devils and casting out devils are bringing down the Kingdom rulership of satan over nations or Kingdoms and people. Demons cannot cast out demons even as miracles, signs and wonders take the power of God. (See Matthew 12:25-26; 24:24). Therefore, we must watch out for false miracles, signs and wonders in the last days or end-times. Counterfeiting is part of deception and lies to confuse and distract the unsuspecting victims. Always, until you discover that you are in bondage, you may never seek for deliverance. Deliverance is the children's bread, but you must ask to receive, seek to find and knock for the door to be opened to you. (See Matthew 7:7). Freedom is for you, so ask the LORD God to set you free from spirit husband, wife, boyfriend, and girlfriend!

Prayers Against Spirit Wives/Husbands

Father, in the name of Jesus Christ, I repent on behalf of myself and those in my family line who have had sexual relations with evil spirits, familiar spirits, dead human spirits, incubus/succubus spirits, and the demon who causes nightmares and works along with sex demons. I ask that the blood of Jesus will cover me as I pray this prayer. I renounce and break any covenant or dedications to the Nephilim, Lilith, Baal or Belial, Cleopatra, Isis, or

Asherah. You can call out or name particular spirits that apply to your personal situation. Father, forgive us for rejecting You as our Husband and for our unfaithfulness towards you. Forgive us for finding comfort from these spirits and for looking to them to fulfill our desires and needs. I choose to rely and trust in You for everything I need. Please restore my joy and faithfulness to the Bridegroom. I take authority over and bind every sexual demon assigned to my tongue, hands, fingers, breasts, hips, lower back, buttocks, sexual organs or any other parts of my body, in the Name of Jesus Christ of Nazareth. I will no longer serve fallen deities in any way, shape or form. Father, close all un-godly pathways, portals, cracks or seams into un-godly realms or the underworld. Lord Jesus, please remove all defilement, pollution and tainting to my spirit, soul and body, in Jesus mighty name. Amen!

Every sin that a man doeth is without the body; but he that committeth fornication sinneth against his own body. What? know ye not that your body is the temple of the Holy Ghost which is in you, which ye have of God, and ye are not your own? For ye are bought with a price: therefore glorify God in your body, and in your spirit, which are God's (1 Corinthians 6:18-20).

Chapter Three

DANGEROUS SOUL-TIES

This is a major reason to teach abstinence -- or sexual immorality and impurity to your children to preserve their lives from defilement and pollution. A soul-tie is a tie that is formed between the soul of a person or animal besides other areas of soul-ties. Soul-ties can be formed when the mind, will and emotions are intertwined and connected. However, a sex-tie is an intimate bond and it is formed through sexual intercourse. We can form "Godly" as well as "ungodly" soul-ties with our family, friends, pastors, churches, doctors, nurses, hospitals, and doctor's offices. One can create a soul-tie with Masonic groups, Boy Scouts, Girl Scouts, sororities, and fraternities, unholy vows or oaths, teachers, instructors, clubs, workplaces and co-workers, etc.

In 1 Samuel 18:1, when David had finished speaking to Saul, *the soul of Jonathan was knit with the soul of David, and Jonathan loved him as his own life.*

Genesis 34:2, 3 said, *And when Shechem son of Hamor the Hivite, Prince of the Country, saw her, he seized her, lay with her, and humbled, defiled, and disgraced her. But his soul longed for and clung to Dinah daughter of Jacob, and he loved the girl and spoke comfortingly to her young heart's wishes.*

Soul-ties are exactly what they sound like. According to 1 Thessalonians 5:23, man is made up of three parts: spirit, soul and body. Every person you connect with in your spirit -- within your heart through thought projection, your mind -- in your imagination, your will and emotionally or through physical bodily contact, a part of you becomes joined together -- glued to that person. Some of us have glued ourselves to all kinds of people through fornication, adultery, and other illicit sexual behaviors. This is why many lives are tormented because the souls are all interconnected inside of each person involved. The situation can get even deeper when the person you share sexual intercourse with, have demons inside their bodies. You also connect to those evil spirits – opening the door of your life to what is clinically believed to be bipolarism, multiple personalities, and schizophrenia. When we fail to break free from soul-ties, they will work perpetually to destroy our future relationships.

When a soul-tie is formed, a person takes on the characteristics of the individual or thing it has formed that tie with. Multiple personalities can simply be that fragmented souls of others are existing on the inside of another. It could also mean that demonic spirits are inhabiting the life of a person and therefore, exhibiting their characteristic behaviors. Deuteronomy 10:20 says, *you shall reverently fear the LORD your God; you shall serve Him and cling to Him, and by His name and presence you shall swear.* The words "cling" or "cleave" means to cling or adhere, fast together, or be joined together. We are to join ourselves to the LORD, and this is an extremely important step in our daily warfare and deliverance. We must endeavor to commit ourselves to the LORD and serve Him. As the tie or oneness is achieved, we will then be able to say like Jesus, *"I and My Father are One."* (See John 10:30).

We can form a soul-tie with just about anyone or anything. I must admonish you to check around your life to see if there is anything controlling your life. This is an indication you have a soul-tie. Do you have something that you just cannot let go? It can be something like a special blanket or trinket. You can recognize a soul-tie by looking into anything that has power over you -- anything you cannot depart from or part ways. This is why the LORD calls us out unto separation!

I plead with every reader today to keep your purity and to teach your children the principles of living chaste and holy lifestyles. The battle over breaking your soul free is not an easy task. Soul-tie is truly a life of torment and torture. The good news is that Jesus Christ is the Deliverer! The Bible said, *He was manifested that He might destroy the works of the devils* (1 John 3:8). The process to gain your freedom may be different from the next person; however, I must assure you that you are going to fight to be made free. You must carefully guard the gates of your life from further intrusion and invasion of the enemy.

Remember that ungodly ties can be formed no matter how much you love and worship the LORD. If you allow your soul to get entangled, you will have to fight for your wholeness through spiritual purging and by breaking the ties. When you undress her in your mind, you are creating an unhealthy soul-tie whether you know it or not! This is why the bible says, to bring every thought captive to the obedience of Christ.

Any thought that exalts itself higher than the word of God, you are responsible to seize or detain and cast it down:

For though we walk in the flesh, we do not war after the flesh: (For the weapons of our warfare are not carnal, but mighty through God to the pulling down of strong holds;) Casting down imaginations, and every high thing that exalteth itself against the knowledge of God, and bringing into captivity every thought to the obedience of Christ (2 Corinthians 10:3-5).

You can look and lust in your heart and commit adultery and fornication without even physically touching a person! Soul ties are extremely powerful:

But I say unto you, that whosoever looketh on a woman to lust after her hath committed adultery with her already in his heart (Matthew 5:28).

Having eyes full of adultery, and that cannot cease from sin; beguiling unstable souls: a heart they have exercised with covetous practices; cursed children (2 Peter 2:14).

What you do with your heart and with your eyes are extremely important:

Job said, *he made a COVENANT with his eyes why then should he think upon a maid!?* (Job 31:1 KJV)

For all that is in the world, the lust of the flesh, and the lust of the EYES and the pride of life, is not of the Father, but is of the world (1 John 2:16).

What you refuse to tame and control will eventually control you! You must be adamant about keeping your soul from being spotted and defiled:

For out of the heart proceed evil thoughts, murders, adulteries, fornications, thefts, false witness, blasphemies (Matthew 15:19).

In this sex crazed and saturated society everywhere you turn today sex scenes are plastered for your eye gates to download the scenes into your soul! You must become the guard of your eyes at all times. Satan knows men are sight stimulated and he will use everything he can to get you on the wrong path and to destroy your relationship with God!

Our hearts must be purified by the refiner's fire. Most times, God will keep us in the flames to purify every centimeter of our hearts so that there are no spots, stains or blemishes that will hinder what He has for us! It is up to us not to jump out of the fire too soon before His works are completed in us!

Another way that our souls are connected to others is through unconscious initiation. Someone, perhaps a parent or relative offered your life on a demonic altar as a collateral for something they were seeking to achieve in life. They may consult spiritual authorities and powers for help and open their lives to satan. This can create multiple problems in your life. It can lead to many difficult and exhausting battles because of what the witch, warlock or satanist had projected upon your life. Let me say this, some soul-ties are harder to break than the others, and it is where the cases become more complex. Therefore, we must look deeper for the legal grounds by the inspiration of the Holy Spirit and revelation of God to successfully break off the ties. It is like excavating hidden tunnels to gather pertinent details that will help to set the soul free from the captors. There are different regions of captivity in the realms of the spirit!

Breaking soul-ties can start off with a basic prayer to disconnect the soul-ties, but it will take a deeper approach depending on how deep a person's case may be, as well as how many partners you've had. Some people have more mileage and it won't just be a 1, 2, 3 step formula. Some things may yield to prayer alone depending on your level of bondage, some will definitely take fasting and some others, you will need help from a trusted leader who has a certain grace in the area you are seeking help for.

What I am teaching you here is that sex is beyond physical contact, sex is SPIRITUAL! It is a bonding that is not easily broken even when the relationship expires! Sex connects your soul energies to another. Therefore, the fragmented soul can be in hundreds of places depending on how many partners you are giving your soul to. You become ONE in the spiritual realm every time you allow someone to penetrate your body.

Spiritual deposits and withdrawals are real and can be devastating to the spirit, soul and body. You must know what you are doing with your body at all times. When you are careless in this area, your life can be shattered and scattered into multiple pieces and it will take you longer periods to fight to get it back! Soul-ties are real! Keep your doors closed and guard the gates of your soul!

Prayers for Breaking Destructive Soul-Ties:

Heavenly Father, I confess and repent of every sin that caused an ungodly soul-tie(s), such as adultery or fornication, masturbation, pornography, etc. And I ask that you forgive me of these sins, iniquities, transgressions and trespasses. Now, you must begin to get rid of any physical gifts or other objects that could hold the soul-tie together, such as a gift given in an illicit or illegitimate relationship. Anything that could hold the tie in place or connected, you definitely want to get them out of your house and away from your life. No matter the cost or value of the gifts, you must know that by retaining them in your possession or custody will hold the bond together between you and that person.

In the name of Jesus Christ and by the power of the blood that was shed to redeem humanity, I ask to be disconnected from every tie that binds my soul with any and all persons, animals, idols, places, objects, subjects and things, etc. In the name of Jesus Christ and by the power of the blood, I now renounce, denounce, break and sever all the soul-ties, and I command my soul to be disconnected in the realms of the spirit from any negative energy streaming through my life. I command all evil spirits to depart from my life in the name of Jesus. Here, you must begin to call out all the names of those you've shared sexual contacts with, or created a soul-tie through the mind, will and emotions. I command all spirits that have taken advantage of this unholy vow to leave me now, in Jesus's name. I also renounce and denounce all involvement with unhealthy (demonic) music that opened me to create soul-ties with the artist who created the music and the demons that influence them to write the music.

Father, I ask for the blood of Jesus Christ to purify my entire life and deliver my soul from every negative tie and curse that has caused me to be hindered, bound and broken. I ask that my fragmented soul will be put back together the way God designed it to be. Father, I ask that you will restore the ground that the enemy has taken advantage of as a result of unhealthy soul-ties. I declare in the name of Jesus Christ that all soul-ties are breaking and coming out now. LORD, I ask that You would heal everywhere I was broken and every curse that has been laid upon my life. I erase myself by the blood of Jesus Christ from the curse of every error and I remove myself from every limitation, in Jesus name.

I ask for God's Warrior Angels to take their swords and completely sever each and every type of soul-tie attachment that has been connected to me from each of those sexual partners, so that I will no longer take on the consequence of their sins, or any penalty from my prior involvement with them.

Here is an important piece of advice: our daily prayers help to break all fresh ties to our lives each day, and gives us the opportunity to name specific people or situations that needs to be revisited, addressed or contended with. You must continuously pray to keep yourself sealed and protected from the curses, ties and other attachments that operate around us. Periodically, you may feel the leading of the Holy Spirit to engage in such prayers again and again! This is the secret of maintaining your deliverance on a daily basis!

But the salvation of the righteous is of the LORD: he is their strength in the time of trouble. And the LORD shall help them, and deliver them: he shall deliver them from the wicked, and save them, because they trust in him (Psalms 37:39-40).

Chapter Four

FREEDOM FROM MASTURBATION

G od is looking to purge our foundation from every-thing that hinders or delays our progress. Some of our roots historically have been tied to Venus and Ashtoreth worship. There are many spiritual roots that stands as open doors through art, idolatry and many forms of elemental spiritual practices. Venus is a Roman god-dess whose functions encompassed love, beauty, desire, sex, fertility, prosperity and victory. Venus was central to many religious festivals and was revered in Roman reli-gion under numerous cult titles.

Many are unaware that illegal sex is worship to idols and demons. When we violate God's principles and laws, the spiritual world is ready to take advantage of our ig-norance or disobedience. Many of our ancestors includ-ing some of us have consciously or unconsciously partici-pated in worship of goddesses and deities other than the True Living God. Our wombs as women must be purged as well as our body parts that participated in labial elonga-tion which comes under the definition of female mastur-bation in order to stretch the female labia minora and this practice opens the door for Kundalini, a powerful demon-ic spirit. It is also called sex-magic or tantra. It activates

Kundalini energy and opens the door for the flooding of lust and perverse marine or water spirits into our lives. Witches call this practice the ultimate blasphemy against God. Masturbation is the awakening of Kundalini without a partner.

Masturbation is a sexual act or conduct performed by a person – man or woman to fulfill, satisfy and achieve the climax of sexual ecstasy. Masturbation cannot be deducted – separated or exempt from sexual sin because sex is given within the framework of God-ordained marriage relationship. Sex outside marriage is fornication and adultery, and sex is part of sacrifice and spiritual worship. Sexual sin is against the body; therefore, the contact is opening our lives to sexual transmitted diseases and demonic pollution and defilement.

Our body as the temple of God must remain pure – sanctified and consecrated and made holy unto the LORD. Polluting and defiling the temple can lead to sudden destruction, not only by the LORD but also the demonic powers besides other sexual complications. All forms of sexual activities whether homosexuality, lesbianism, bestiality, fornication, adultery, molestation, rape, incest and sodomy are detested by the LORD. The use of sex objects, materials, computer, phone, magazine and other stimulating tools to create virtual sexual contact or engage in sexual act is venturing into a forbidden boundary.

There are many factors that can drive a person's sexual appetite, but understanding the boundary is the key to limiting the passion from accelerating into lustful and pervasive overdrive. Lust, perversion, fantasy, loneliness, emotional damage and selfish desires can open one's life to masturbation and pornography. Lust enters through the eye-gate, to develop the image or picture within the mind and the mind, will, and emotion influence our lives and actions. Our eye-gates must be closed and carefully guarded besides repenting of every sexual involvement whether it be masturbation, pornography or otherwise. Our surroundings are equally important in escaping from sexual temptation. Cleaning up our environments can help expedite our deliverance from demonic powers. The Bible said, *I will set no wicked thing before my eyes* (Psalms 101:3). Exposing yourself to materials, objects, subjects, instruments, tools, pictures, images, videos, communication and environments that produce and promote sexual curiosity -- induce sexual contact will stimulate or arouse sexual attraction and affection. You need to withdraw and purposefully distance yourself! You must flee sexual sin! Sin and judgment are like law and order!

Fantasy is not a mere delusion but using the mind to creatively achieve a desired goal. The world is consumed by the illusion of fantasy and the spirit realms use deception to enslave the human race. The mind creates mental pictures or graphical images and the person engaging in masturbation may envision and use the focus of the mind to initiate the interaction. The animation gives the images life and the connection leads to virtual reality experience. What people may not understand is that the use of the mind to connect can present a false realty of anyone and anything the mind focuses on, as a contact. The dream of sharing real sexual contact with an imaginary partner often leads to false conviction. This opens one up to immediate contact with the spiritual world.

The Bible said, *For though we walk in the flesh, we do not war after the flesh: (For the weapons of our warfare are not carnal, but mighty through God to the pulling down of strong holds;) Casting down imaginations, and every high thing that exalts itself against the knowledge of God, and bringing into captivity every thought to the obedience of Christ* (2 Corinthians 10:4-5).

Fantasy is going beyond a personal assessment or estimation of having a secured contact and interaction because the mind is part of the spiritual life. Venturing into the spirit realms is connecting with spirit beings even when the pictures we painted in our imaginations have no identities attached or associated with them. The spirit realms are so fast that it takes a moment to come into proximity with the spirit world. Lust and fantasy are represented by spirits, which is to say that our minds must be renewed and our hearts must be circumcised in the spirit. (See Romans 12:2; Ezekiel 11:19; 36:26; 44:9). Therefore, masturbation is not having sex with oneself but sharing intercourse with foreign entities. The way to deal with false – evil spirits is to cast them out. Our lives must be sanctified and consecrated: we must return to the word of God and open our lives to the outpouring of the Holy Spirit until we achieve whole transformation. These processes are the keys to breaking the power of masturbation.

The way to protect your thought life is by the word of God and the Spirit of God. We need the Word as we need the life and power of God actively working in our lives:

Thy word have I hid in my heart that I might not sin against thee (Psalms 119:11).

Create in me a clean heart Oh God and renew a right spirit in me (Psalms 51:10).

Besides renewing our mind, we can have the mind of Christ through the Spirit of Christ:

Searching what, or what manner of time the Spirit of Christ (1 Peter 1:11).

Let this mind be in you, which was also in Christ Jesus (Philippians 2:5).

There are damaged emotions as a result of bitter end of relationships. Verbal abuse, sexual abuse and inferiority complexes can lead to lasting spiritual and physical wounds and injuries. People will say things like: I wish I would have never come in contact with you or I hate you for life. You will never find any other person like me or no one loves me. The effect of rape, molestation, sodomy, incest abuse and other forms of sexual abuses can open the doors to deep spiritual hurts and pains. When these issues become the root cause of masturbation, the demon spirit attached to the mind and emotion – the soul must be cast out.

To break the spirit of masturbation will take an extended work of the Holy Spirit. If a person's life has been impacted by incest abuse, raped, or other sexual abuse related cases, the spirits of anger, rage, hostility, fear, hatred and many more have to be cast out during deliverance. The perpetrators or violators must be forgiven and it may take counseling and conviction of the Holy Spirit to soften the individual's determination to avenge the incident. Damaged emotions can lead to social withdrawal, seclusion and distrust like when Tamar was raped by her half-brother. (See 2 Samuel Chapter 13). When the root of masturbation is damaged emotions, the wound is deeper than the sexual act. We must know that such deliverance takes great commitment and dedication, not a quick remedy. The Bible said, this kind goes not out except by fasting and prayer (Matthew 17:21). Realizing total victory will take progressive efforts until full deliverance is achieved! The good news is that you can be free!

Loneliness can lead people to masturbation and they may consciously explore the option to satisfy their sexual desires. The way to deal with loneliness is to have a vibrant personal fellowship with the LORD besides involving yourself in different activities even if it is volunteering. The void of life is not a matter of material satisfaction nor filling all our feelings and sensations. The spiritual is what offsets the natural appetite to mortify the deeds of the flesh. (See Romans 8:13; Colossians 3:5). You must think on those things which are pure. (See Philippians 4:8; Titus 1:15). Cast down all negative imagination. (See 2 Corinthians 10:3-5). Listen to godly music, read the word of God, fast and pray, keep away from sexual content materials that are stimulants to sexual lust and perversion. Sanctify and consecrate your environment. Ask the LORD to release your marital partner and help you connect the right way. (See 1 Thessalonians 2:8; 1 Timothy 2:15).

Some people have been affected negatively by past relationships and they avoid taking another step to involve in any new relationship. Some people do not want the challenges of having to deal with anything relationship. Some people out of suspicion and distrust cannot welcome or cultivate a relationship; it's simply too much hassle or restriction. And they can mistake being single as a resolution. However, they may carelessly embrace masturbation or pornography as ways to confront their sexual frustration. They may not see masturbation and pornography as sexual sins that can open their lives to different problems.

To be free, they must submit their will to the Holy Spirit and undergo through deliverance. Of course, they must repent of masturbation and pornography, learn the word of God, and they must forgive.

Besides great number of people engaging in masturbation and pornography everywhere around the world, masturbation is not talked about openly, especially among Christians that are bound by masturbation. For the addiction of masturbation to be broken and defeated, the victims must not hide or remain silent. Masturbation as in dealing with all sins, must be confessed and repented before prayer of deliverance and freedom can be realized. The LORD loves His people but He hates the sins of the people, which is why He died on the cross to save them.

When people are no longer able to control the urge to masturbate or watch pornography, it is certain that demonic entities have invaded their sex lives. Using the power of imagination to simulate the reality of what is not there, is in real sense attracting what we imagine into our lives. When you imagine having sex with someone while masturbating or watching pornography, you are summoning spiritual powers to manifest what you are imagining. You may have heard about the law of attraction, made popular from books and movies like "The Secret." There is such thing as sex demons of sexual lust and perversion!

Jesus said, *But I say unto you, that whosoever looketh on a woman to lust after her hath committed adultery with her already in his heart* (Matthew 5:28).

The danger of masturbation is that a person can inadvertently summon or invite demonic spirits to attach themselves – cleave to his or her life. This is how demons claim to be married to people, so there are spirit husbands and wives as well as spirit boyfriends and girl-friends. What they are doing is mimicking the different characteristic behaviors exhibited in the respective relationships. The challenge however is that once demons attach themselves to people, it is difficult to force them to leave except through extensive deliverance to be set free. When you are pressured with the urge to masturbate or watch pornography, the power can become too compelling that in your struggle to achieve orgasm, you will find yourself being bound in captivity. Every time you experiment and achieve temporary relief, another wave will hit you. Demons attract the likes besides purposefully opening the door for other demons to enter because it is all about embarking upon the Kingdom assignments. It is the reason people can collect so many demons without knowing. Once the demons enter, they will work to secure their webs of control over your life to make it extremely harder to get free.

When the unclean spirit is gone out of a man, he walketh through dry places, seeking rest, and findeth none. Then he saith, I will return into my house from whence I came out; and when he is come, he findeth it empty, swept, and garnished. Then he goes, and taketh with himself seven other spirits more wicked than himself, and they enter in and dwell there: and the last state of that man is worse than the first. Even so shall it be also unto this wicked generation (Matthew 12:43-45)

By opening yourself and engaging in sexual impurity, you are giving evil spirits the legal access or the right to intrude into your life. These demons can remain in your life – causing untold personal pain, hurt, guilt, and shame until they are cast out. (See Luke 8:29; 9:39, 42; 2 Corinthians 6:17-18).

Pornography: even people who have practiced Christianity for long time struggle with pornography and masturbation. Evil tendencies can begin in a very early stage of life, so those frequenting the adult sites, bookstores, or view adult videos may have not started as adults. Some might have been exposed in the early stages of life either by family members, relatives, or through contact with pornographic materials. There is a correlation between pornography and masturbation because everything is about contaminating or infecting the eye-gate. The Bible may not have spoken about masturbation emphatically; however, masturbation is one branch of sexuality. Therefore, we must be thorough in addressing everything sexuality to expose the enemy's hidden agenda when it comes to lust and perversion in our generation. Whether masturbation is engaged through eye contact with external materials or imaginary conception, sexual act involves a sexual partner, and anything sexual must fall into line with the defined order of martial law. Lust and perversion are outside of the confines of both spiritual and physical laws of marriage and sex.

Demons have no age preference, so children are targeted even in the sex industries today besides other numerous sexual solicitations involving the opposite and same sex partners. Animals and nature are also targeted with sexual pollution to indicate that the abnormal order – the inordinate and wrongful attraction are not mistaken concepts, but separate entities fanning the flames. All aspects of sexual contacts are consolidated to show strict regulation and violating the principles incur great damage to our lives. Fornication, adultery, homosexuality, lesbianism, bestiality, bisexuality, and omnisexuality, all involves corroborating partnership and to misunderstand masturbation as only a personal act involving oneself is a gross misdiagnosis.

Soul-ties and spirits are united together through sexual contacts – similar to two people consummating a lawful marriage. There is no aspect of sex that is safe outside the confines of the rules. Sexual gratification is not the most important part of sexuality, but following the rules that safeguard from the penalty of sexual misconducts. The obligation of the law is a mandatory restriction and all opinions are not alternatives to fulfilling the law. If lust towards a man or woman can be treated as sexual contact, every other aspect of sexual contact cannot be ignored. They fit together in the same box to show the expansion of all sexual behaviors. The targeted audience of sexual immorality is not limited to a special group because lust and perversion have not selection. The Bible remedy for sexual immorality is to flee.

And likewise also the men, leaving the natural use of the woman, burned in their lust one toward another; men with men working that which is unseemly, and receiving in themselves that recompence of their error which was meet (Romans 1:27).

Chapter Five

CHEATING SPOUSES

Sexually loose husbands are everywhere these days. Many of them arrogantly expose the knowledge of the other women to their wives and yet, keep everything away from the scrutinizing eyes of the larger society. Of course, the cases of cheating husbands are not a new phenomenon in many societies around the world. What is of great concern is the high level of arrogance with which some men are involving in immorality today, and their wives are totally complacent or simply not able to do anything about it, so they stay mute.

Many of the women who are married to these promiscuous men are aware of their husbands' unfaithfulness, nevertheless, they remain committed to the marriages and keep silent about the infidelity of their spouses. Most of the women do not want to expose their shame and embarrassment, so they choose to stay committed to the deceitful relationships.

In fact, evidences are documented in several blogs and websites about the multiple irregularities of famous sexually loose husbands who take undue advantage of their wives while cheating with other women. What's more worrisome is that in many instances, some of these women have been pacified and conditioned to lie in defense of their adulterous husbands. Consequently, some of these subdued wives are languishing behind the closed doors of guilt and despair. Many of these women are now living under the shadows -- risking their health, well-being and losing their self-esteem and confidence in the process.

The great challenge today is that these lifestyles are very much active in the houses of worship and virtually practiced among prominent leaders of different Church groups or organizations. There are so many sexually loose husbands that are salivating and begging for extra-marital sex with promissory notes or incentive offers across the world. They have corrupted their lives and ministries and every day; they are working additionally harder to clean up their tracks and hide the evidences from the general public. However, the age of technologies has made it impossible to hide behind the clouds of deception and lies today.

I want you to learn how to uncoil your life and unchain your purpose and destiny from the snares and tentacles of adultery through this epic spiritual and practical guide. I am praying that many people will embrace the courage and confidence to release the spirit of adultery and break the binding-ruling power over their lives and households. The spirit of betrayal is commissioned and delegated to reduce the moral sanctity of your marriage to a mere defiled sanctuary.

Lovers must understand self-sacrifice or it's only a package and baggage of lust. There is no worship without holiness; therefore, gifts are not the alternative expression of the life of love. Love is a life poured out in honor or memorial so there is no duplicity or distributed affections and attractions. Marital love is tailored-fit for a husband and a wife, and when we create illegitimate extensions to apportion love to outside seekers, we destroy the faithfulness and loyalty to sacrifice our lives like Christ died for the Church. This is an abortion or hemorrhage of love. Inordinate affection is a breach of divine order – so it's interfering with or trespassing into forbidden territories by violating the oath of marital vows. Lack of love is a dishonor of the marriage vow, which is why the compensation of great material gifts never heal the wounds of broken love relationships. The oath of marriage is not an addendum, but a constitutional instrument created by the Institutor of marriage.

Marriage is standing before God in eternal oath so our witnesses and testimonies of infidelities are bad records in our marital report cards. Marriage without love is like a life without blood or spirit! The Spirit is the air that propels life in the spirit realm, even as blood is the fuel that fans the rhythm of the physical life. The appropriation of love according to divine order will heal the memories of hurtful marital abuses or the wounds will open to rejection and welcome the torment of oppression. Wrongful relationships only breed the ground for hurt and pain, and the roots increase and multiply the effects that will negatively impact future generations.

The questions anyone reading this chapter would want to ask are:

1. Why on earth would any woman subject herself to such open humiliation in the hand of someone who proclaimed to love her?
2. What could be responsible for this abnormality?

3. Why are women subjecting themselves to unhealthy abuses and non-dignifying marital conditions?

Let me briefly share with you some of the reasons why some women are choosing to remain in such unhealthy relationships, despite the psychological and emotional trauma they experience on regular basis. Afterwards, I will show you some tested and trusted approaches through which women can break free from the psychological and spiritual deficiencies caused by unholy compromised marriages.

Why do women remain committed to adulterous relationships?

Ideally, no woman in her right senses would want to share her husband with the other women. He is a sacred property belonging only to her and vice versa. So, when a woman gives up her defense to put up with a serial womanizer without raising her voice, then something is fundamentally wrong. There are several factors why a woman would want to tolerate a sexually loose husband.

Here are some of such factors:

1. **Lack of Self-esteem:** Many women who stay in such abuses are lacking self-esteem and true spiritual confidence. Such women see themselves as being inferior and less worthy, so, whatever their husbands are doing cannot be questioned. Some of these women even consider themselves lucky to have married such a man who could have gone for someone they consider to be better than them. In these kinds of homes, the husbands are lords, and their decisions, including going out with other

women, are unquestionable. The wife believes she has no say, and thereby accepts the situation as her fate.

2. **Shame from Social Stigma**: Some women, because of the fear and shame of what people will say if they find out their husbands are cheating on them, have simply decided to go mute about their husbands' extra-marital affairs. This is a self-inflicted injury. These women will continue to suffer the trauma and agony alone behind closed doors as they constantly make efforts to hide the true reality of their relationships from friends and family members, who could have perhaps offered a helping hand. The husbands will definitely take advantage of their silence and continue deeper into their adulterous lifestyles unabated.

3. **Fear of Divorce**: Due to the fear of social stigmatization that is always associated with the status of divorced women in most societies around the world, women often shy away from any conditions that might trigger a separation and divorce. Therefore, to avoid the incident, many women do everything, including enduring their husbands' infidelity. So many women have lost their energies, well-beings, self-esteem and confidence.

4. **Fear of Financial Security**: Many women who are married to successful sexually loose husbands cannot sacrifice their outlandish lifestyles and quit the relationships because their sustainability depends heavily on the man's wealth. Thus, for the fear of not losing their financial security, these women prefer to suffer great internal struggle. The epidemic of extra-marital affairs is so open today that some high-class marriages are devalued with compromised gifts to pacify and take away the rights of

the vulnerable wives to oppose or reject the loose husbands' immoral disability and dysfunctionality.

5. **For the sake of their kids**: It is also common to see women who could not bear to have their children live without a father-figure make resolutions to remain with sexually loose husbands. They believe it is better for them to sacrifice their own happiness for the good of their children. This might not be the best option! There are countless women who have chosen to live solitary and unfulfilling lives for the sake of their children's well-being.

6. **Lack of Spiritual Authority and Power:** When a woman lacks spiritual authority and power, she might also be lacking the strength to battle some of the challenges of life, thereby compromising her marriage with a spiritually deficient husband. Such women languish in lamentations and sorrows resulting from the nonchalant attitudes of their husbands without knowing the way forward or how to liberate themselves from the marital bondage.

The above-mentioned factors are only some of the reasons many women are subjecting their lives to untold abuses from sexually loose husbands without making any meaningful efforts to fight back or at least seek a separation and divorce to liberate themselves. In reality, none of the reasons mentioned above is potent enough to make a woman compromise her happiness – spiritual and physical well-being. If you are a woman enduring an adulterous relationship because you are afraid of being alone and poor, or fear of shame and embarrassment, I want to tell you that you're losing more (your entire life) by remaining in an unhealthy relationship. I want you to know that with a good support system through friends and family, many women have been able to create an active and a meaningful social life without an adulterous spouse until the LORD sent them the right husbands.

The Way Out

The essence of this chapter is to help you to liberate yourself from indecent and unfulfilling relationships. The plan of God for you is to build a fulfilling marital life. Anything short of this is not acceptable if you are a true child of God. Therefore, wake up to reality. Come to your right senses and demand your right. You should never settle for less! Your goal is to establish a godly relationship with your husband without a third party standing in-between you and what is your sacred proprietary blessing.

If you are reading this book and you have been locked up in an adulterous relationship. If your husband is a serial womanizer who does not have regards for your person. If you have been wallowing in self-pity, regretting why you have chosen to marry your sexually loose husband. It's time you consider a better alternative to your present life. I challenge you today to take steps towards liberating yourself. Activate your life again and quit living in the shadow of the man who does not really care for your spiritual and physical life.

Here are some of the things you need to do if you really want to liberate yourself from any relationship that is filled with emotional torture and agony:

1. **You must Present Your Husband with the Facts:** If you really love your husband, your first response should be to try to salvage the relationship before doing anything drastic. You should not act on impulse alone, but instead gather your facts and pres-

ent your husband with the facts. Allow him to tell his own side of the story. Stand tall and tell him to his face where you're sure he is lying. As long as he is not abusing you physically or verbally, give him some time to decide if he is going to come out clean for the interest of the relationship or if he will continue in his adulterous lifestyle.

2. **Talk to a Professional Relationship Counselor:** It is emotionally and psychologically draining if you find out that your husband is engaging in extra-marital affair. So, it is important that you get a professional (spiritual and physical) help at this stage. It does not matter whether your husband quits the extra-marital affairs or not, you need a relationship counselor to walk you through the overwhelming and emotional challenging situation. Prayerfully work with the counselor to see what options are still available for you in your relationship. While you are working with the relationship counselor, keep studying your husband's actions to see if he wants to move on with or without you. Do not be afraid of the worst-case scenario. You must know that adultery is a biblical ground for divorce.

3. **Decide When to Give Up:** No matter how much you love your husband, you must also love yourself. If he is not ready to turn a new leaf and quit his adulterous lifestyle, you will have to give up on him for the sake of your own well-being. You should not continue to care for someone who does not give a concern about your own emotional feelings or spiritual and physical state. You should not abide outrightly with infidelity for the sake of anything including your children. It is not even recommended that you raise your children in such a home where your dignity is not valued and respected. You

have a better chance to raise your children in the way you want them to go (in the way of the LORD) when you are emotionally and mentally stable than in a home where your emotions are being trampled and abused on a regular basis. It is "living in bondage" to stay with a sexually loose husband because of his wealth or any other benefits. So, if he chooses not to mend his ways and approach the relationship with a genuine intention to reconcile with you, it's time to give him an ultimatum and move on.

4. **Give an Ultimatum and Be Ready to Move On:** If your husband fails to stop his adulterous lifestyle despite all your efforts to remedy the situation, it's time to disengage. Remaining in such relationship will not help you in any way. You must protect your life from further deterioration. It is not possible for you to continue in a relationship with a third party wedged in the middle. Remaining in such relationship will torment you psychologically and emotionally and leave you both spiritually and morally bankrupt. It will hinder and dwarf your spiritual growth and maturity and destroy your purpose and destiny in life. There are so many women who have contracted sexually transmitted diseases and demons. This is very unfortunate!

5. **Consider Starting a New Life:** There is always a new beginning – a time of fresh renewal. A season and moment to move things forward – take a new step. Do not sit down to wallow in self-pity, shame, or regret. Consult with your counselor on the way forward and prayerfully focus on a new career or path of life. The most important thing is your own freedom. You cannot flourish and fulfill your purpose and destiny if you remain in a relationship that

is spiritually deficient. Spiritual deficiency gives birth to physical paralysis!

I must admonish you not to remain in an adulterous relationship that continues to degrade your life as a sensible human being. I know that many of you who are reading this material can identify with a form of oppression. We are supposed to live free of any and all forms of bondage; that includes our mistakes from the past, our present failures and unpleasant memories. Therefore, when the LORD sets you free from any kind of bondage, never pick up the chain again! Leave the broken chains where they are fallen off and quickly, move on.

Women, God made you for a special purpose: *For you are God's workmanship, created in Christ Jesus to do good works, which God prepared in advance for us to do* (Ephesians 2:10).

You are the product of God and God is jealous over you. The scriptures tell us that a husband should deal with his wife very delicately -- according to (divine) knowledge, not ignorantly or foolishly to avoid hindrances to your prayers. (See 1 Peter 3:7). It is no joking matter! Husbands, be considerate as you live with your wives, and treat them with respect as the weaker partner and as heirs of the gracious gift of life.

The LORD wants men to understand from spiritual perspective that, the woman is not a sex toy. She is a to be adored and loved as you love your own physical body. He who loves his wife, loves himself. The Bible said, *woman is the glory of the man* (1 Corinthians 11:7). God steps in to defend women when they are misused in any society or culture.

When we begin to understand the depths of Scriptures, our family love lives will start to transform. Remember, that transformation is greater than change! Marriage is a divine arrangement, and not an earthly or man-made contract arrangement. Love is a secret life, but it is celebrated in the open. There is no conflict of interest in God-ordained marriage because of perfected order! When things are out of order, some things will start to hemorrhage. It is out of order when we pollute and defile the marriage bed and break our marital covenant agreements.

The man who cannot bring his sexual appetite under control is under bondage of compulsive sexual lust and perversion. We must mortify the deeds of the flesh if we are going to please God and honor our marriage covenant. Romans 8:13 said, For if we live after the flesh, ye shall die. But if he through the spirit do mortify the deeds of the body, he shall live. Submitting to the dictations and agitations of the flesh will degrade our lives, lower our personality and turn us into adult delinquent.

King Solomon was the wisest man on Earth in his day. The Bible said, God gave him the wisdom of all wise men that were before him, and there were great wise men who lived thousands of years prior to his time. Although Solomon had unequaled wisdom, he was seduced by the powerful ruling lust spirit.

1 Kings 11:3-8 recorded the following account: *And he had seven hundred wives, princesses, and three hundred concubines: and his wives turned away his heart. For it came to pass, when Solomon was old, that his wives turned away his heart after other gods: and his heart was not perfect with the LORD his God, as was the heart of David his father. For*

Solomon went after Ashtoreth the goddess of the Zidonians, and after Milcom the abomination of the Ammonites. And Solomon did evil in the sight of the LORD, and went not fully after the LORD, as did David his father. Then did Solomon build an high place for Chemosh, the abomination of Moab, in the hill that is before Jerusalem, and for Molech, the abomination of the children of Ammon. And likewise did he for all his strange wives, which burnt incense and sacrificed unto their gods (1 Kings 11:3-8).

Just as in the past or days of king Solomon, the mighty are falling in our time – many are being brought low because they entertain the same demon known as Ashtoreth. The Bible commanded us to *resist the devil (and his demons) and he will flee.* (See James 4:7b). Today, many people are not resisting the devils. The word of God still stands: people are not fleeing fornication and adulterous relationships, instead they are opening their lives to demonic intrusion!

Some of the greatest preachers are falling away – those who were once influential and traveled the world. Those who were known for wonderful works: miracles, signs and wonders across different nations or kingdoms. So many who are under the same demonic power are seducing and destroying the lives of men and women everywhere.

Another important Bible character is Samson: his life history is recorded in the Book of Judges, Chapters 13 thru 16. He was a Danite. His mother was barren until the Angel of the LORD appeared unto her and told her she would conceive and bear a son. She was given clear instructions on her diet, how to raise up her son, and the manner of life he must live. He was called a Nazarite – a life that is wholly separated unto God and totally dedicated to God's calling. A Nazarite vow or covenant requires a particular oath as a token of sacrifice to God. No razor could touch the hair of Samson all the days of his life. Samson had great power to do things that no mere mortal can do. He was called to the office of a judge over Israel. He judged over Israel for twenty years!

Samson married a Philistine woman, and the relationship ended in a disaster. Then he visited Gaza and spent half the night with a harlot. In spite all of this he still had his strength -- he thought he could have the best of both worlds. We can see clearly from the life of Samson that these powers are no push over. They can instigate the fall of the great and mighty, if they are not careful. In Judges 16:15-21, Delilah came along and finished him off.

1 Corinthians 6:18 said, *Flee Fornication. Every sin that a man doeth is without the body, but he that commits fornication sins against his own body.*

Proverbs 6:32, *But whoso commits adultery with a woman lacks understanding.*

I am praying for those reading through this material for the LORD to help you to know that love is what holds godly relationships upon the tracks of eternal life.

The Bible said, *For God so loved the world that He gave His only begotten Son* (John 3:16).

To the men everywhere, as you give your life to your wife to fit her in her proper place in your life, the blessing of God will be released to fully nurture your marriage. I pray for freedom from generational curses and bloodline proclivities in the life of everyone reading this book, in Jesus name.

Marriage is honourable in all, and the bed undefiled: but whoremongers and adulterers God will judge (Hebrews 13:4).

PROTECTING OUR CHILDREN

We want to retrace the footstep of our forefathers, who lost their places and failed their ultimate commitments and dedication to the LORD God. Always, to worship God takes great personal sacrifices beyond the things we offer as our generous giving for the services of the LORD. The way we conduct ourselves or live our daily lives are extremely important that our future generations can suffer terrible consequences because of our actions. When a child is conceived, he or she is kept protected for nine months of its development in the warm, soft nest of blood in the mother's womb. When the baby is born, he/or she is literally covered by the blood of his/her mother. The little child is born into a blood covenant with his/her parents. The fall of the first man has made it possible for the enemy to target the offspring even before they were born. He does not wait until they have grown to the age of accountability and responsibility.

Thou shalt not bow down thyself unto them, nor serve them: for I the LORD thy God am a jealous God, visiting the iniquity of the fathers upon the children unto the third and fourth generation of them that hate me (Deuteronomy 5:9).

The circle and cycle of bondage is like a cobweb or tentacles that the enemy uses to enclose family lines. The enemy visits every family to investigate the history and to dig up ancestral issues from the bloodlines. The biological and genealogical records are examined to see if the history is clean. There is no way that the human race could have been able to be free from the power of sin and the judgment of sin without the bloodline of Jesus Christ, the Second Adam and Son of God. The people of God must see beyond personal reasons and beliefs because legality is not a matter of our opinions and ideological concepts but having evidential or incriminating proofs. If the proofs relate to a person, a family, a nation or kingdom and people, everyone is held under the cord of the binding consequences without exemptions. The foundation has already been built before the next generation until a different generation rises up to address the stronghold.

The Bible said, *Or else, how can one enter a strong man's house, and spoil his goods, except he first binds the strongman? And then he will spoil his house* (Matthew 12:29).

Because the LORD God visits generational issues in the family line: life is in the blood and every life that come out of the biological bloodline is a target whether the child is born today or yet to be born. The bloodline serves are a criminal history to implicate the whole family line. It is like transferring the family debts to the loved ones and it is not a matter of claiming, confessing and believing to be free without dealing with the problems legally. Some records are not within our jurisdiction so we cannot easily make them go away by wishful thinking. Visiting the iniquity of the fathers on the children did not outline or state that the process begin only after the child is born. Therefore, why would the enemy wait until the birth of the child to attack? We must know that the attacks on the child begins from the womb and in some cases, even before the child is conceived. Some parents go through great pain to have children because of legal spiritual contests. Until the breakthrough comes, there can be no pregnancy and if the pregnancy takes place, different complications will immediately impact the process of bringing forth the child into the world.

A generation is at least ten years, which is to say that many generations are laden with heavy bondage; sometimes, the people are totally ignorant and the record is carried over to generations after generations. Some children are under tremendous pressure from birth and even though they are still under the age of innocence, the enemy has already placed heavy demand upon the life of the child. They will begin to visit the child spiritually and engage the parents is spiritual legal battles for accessibility because of what is in the family bloodline. Sicknesses and diseases, poverty, lack, misfortune, bad luck, failures, and defeats are all parts of spiritual and physical inheritance. Evil inheritances are parts of spiritual implications unless they are legally vacated or dismissed, they will remain active and effective. The enemy does not want the consequences stemming from the parental bloodline issues to be reversed at the peak of the fourth generations: they want to extend the cord indefinitely — without anyone in the family line ever breaking free. Children are under extraordinary pressure, especially in this generation: parental responsibilities are fading and the resistance against the powers of evil in families are dying out. Evil spirits are having their ways in families. Some generational lines are greatly fortified and because families are abandoning their spiritual obligations to fight to free their homes, we are seeing desolation. We are seeing the repetition or circles of bondage in families everywhere.

The battle that went on to protect the life of Jesus Christ before and after birth was more than enough to destroy Him as a little baby. (See Matthew Chapter 2). Angels stepped in and the family fought back. When the battle became more daring, the parents escaped into a different nation. Other children lost their lives in the effort to find Him. Children deal with great spiritual warfare even in the ages of immaturity. Often parents don't know how to protect them through prayers and sacrifices unto the LORD. Agents of darkness with their respective agencies are tasked with hurting innocent children everywhere. Controlling the population is not the only evil agenda of the wicked one — the entire human race is targeted including unborn babes and children. Many children with great purposes and destinies have been destroyed through abortion and other malicious intentions. Families are seen as one and the offspring is seen as one with the family so when the enemy target the family, no one is safe because all family members are pursued.

When we speak about generational curses, we are laying emphasis on passed-down incidents that involved the parents, which resulted in the lives of the children being impacted consequently. Parents, grandparents and great grandparents may have sinned against the LORD God by practicing witchcraft arts, worshiped idols, joined occultist groups, and there may be other behavioral patterns that run in the family line: alcoholism, drug addictions, incest, fornication, pornography, adultery, bestiality, homosexuality, and lesbianism, etc.

We have to understand that the effects of curses are the results of the enforcement. The scripture tells us that the curse causeless can't come. There must be a legal cause for the curses to continue: wherever the curses are released, mixed with whoever is enforcing the curses to bring the fulfillment. This is why it is like a certification to keep the circulation revolving around the family until it is broken to destroy the legal rights. Always, family is established after the nature of God (Galatians 5:22-23), to function without any rejection, hate, envy, addiction, and other diabolical tendencies filtering into the biological and genealogical lines.

Every parent must repent on behalf of the family to keep the generations from hidden problems. The blessings of the parents are the true inheritance of the children. The curses are the opposite of the blessing; therefore, the children need proper family foundations to grow upon and extend without inviting curses on their lives. There must be a continuous prayer, fasting and sacrifices for the children besides raising them up in the fear and admonition of the LORD.

And it was so, when the days of their feasting were gone about, that Job sent and sanctified them, and rose up early in the morning, and offered burnt offerings according to the number of them all: for Job said, It may be that my sons have sinned, and cursed God in their hearts. Thus did Job continually (Job 1:5).

Children can pray and a godly family is an altar of the LORD and the Ministers are the parents like Job, Abraham and many other patriarchs. (See Genesis 21:15-17). God is holding the parents accountable and responsible for their gifts of the womb! Even before they are born, parents must labor to secure their passages into this life and keep their paths from crossing with the enemy. The Bible said, *The thief cometh not, but for to steal, and to kill, and to destroy* (John 10:10a). The fruit of the children are the blessings of the parents and we must be careful not to cast our seeds to the killer and destroyer.

Parents must repent of all personal and family sins and rededicate and commit the family to God — cover the children with prayer and the sprinkling of the blood of Jesus Christ. Teach them the rightful ways of the LORD and protect them from evil covenants and initiations. Children need spiritual supervision and monitoring to keep the evil one away from their lives.

Train up a child in the way he should go: and when he is old, he will not depart from it (Proverbs 22:6).

Chapter Seven

FASTING FOR FREEDOM

Always, I like to emphasize on the key of fasting whether it relates to answers to prayers for healing, deliverance, restitution, reparation, repatriation and restoration, etc. Fasting as a vital component of prayer offers important secrets to an expedited and accelerated process. Spiritual breakthrough comes with tremendous acceleration to break spiritual and physical barriers. To see a sudden or momentary response, there must be a shift — infiltration and penetration of the defensive and security layers prohibiting or protecting the spiritual and physical realms. Fasting is useful and very effective in thinning the walling partition of the human flesh and removing spiritual barricades or blockades. Until the spirit realms come together with the physical realms, the sudden outburst of spiritual phenomena cannot begin to emanate in accelerated speed. What causes people to breakdown and give up are the long periods of waiting and endless expectations for the results of their prayers. They throw in their towels because they feel that nothing is really happening. The same way the atmosphere of expectation breed miracles, lack of results breeds discouragement and disappointment. Empty hope is not a substitute for real answers. This is why religious activities are separate from true Christian experiences. The disciples came to Jesus and asked Him to teach them how to pray.

And it came to pass, that, as he was praying in a certain place, when he ceased, one of his disciples said unto him, Lord, teach us to pray, as John also taught his disciples (Luke 11:1).

Praying and receiving answers to prayers are two different things because formalities are only exhibitions of religious practices with no recipe for definitive outcomes. The activities can become the only hope and people are forced or coerced to embrace empty religion. A dead system is established as an alternative to answer for true spiritual experience but until we carefully discern, estimate and appreciate the deep values of spiritual things beyond assessments, claims and confessions, belief, hope and trust, there can be no real loyalty and faithfulness, which are the key ingredients of spiritual establishment. Empty prayers equal an empty life; therefore, satisfaction cannot be realized in the face of nothing. Building upon false pretense will eventually lead to anxiety, debates and extremism. Always, loyalty and faithfulness are not compatible with falsehood. The things we do not have answers to, are the things we cannot defend and taking the matter into our own hands is violating the spiritual order of life, so there cannot be an establishment. Many religious establishments are setbacks to people's destinies. Principles are parts of the codes to unlock a system or everybody will embark upon religious adventures, often with dangerous consequences. Although fasting is not starving, it is to stave off the human appetite until spiritual transparency and clarity are achieved. To know the will and purpose of God takes more than rehearsing the Bible. There is an aspect of personal knowing — or coming into real spiritual relations and experiences with the LORD God and no number of researches and experimentation can suffice. Any relationship at some point must involve personal interactions besides other engagements depending on the progression before the initial termination. To see the disciples address Jesus by the word "Master" is worthy of re-evaluation. When it comes to religious prayers, there are many experts in our modern days, but when it has to deal with praying and getting answered results, we do not have many masters. We have masters of theology and many other ideological concepts: political, religious, scientific, technological and so forth! The human race is facing a dire moment!

We need those who will pray and make real contact with Heaven beyond touching the fabrics of man-made confusing and distracting systems. Prayer is a spiritual art; however, it is not to say that prayer is ritualistic. It is simply attaining the pinnacle or climax of spiritual communication and dialogue. The most qualified ingredients of prayer are combined sacrifices and communications. The intrigue of prayers cannot be consummated until the answers to prayers begin to make landfalls in our lives. There is no way to keep records of achievements without the evidence of success. Life is not programmed and animated (made/created) to accept complacency as an alternative to real success. Therefore, unanswered prayers create awareness of the loss of invested season, time and efforts. It is why we fight so hard to conceal the records of our failures.

The disciples acknowledged that Jesus was a Master when it comes to praying and seeing manifested and revealed answers. How easy it would be to find people praying everywhere today if answers to their prayers were eminent. There would be protests to keep prayers in the public places rather than to remove prayers from the public places. We are seeing reversions of spiritual orders across the world, not only in times of prayers, but the Church removing prayers from their gathering. We see the focus more on edifices, religious ceremonies and coronations. We see empty benedictions and pronunciations of blessings that never matures or manifest. We are seeing a pattern of the world systems and the Church systems pairing together like uniform codes.

Prayers mixed with fasting are important aspects of our lives as believers. If men ought to pray without fainting or until the answer to prayers are released, we must see the need for fervency, commitment and dedication to prayers and fasting. It is the vehicle and practice that helps catapult our persistence in prayers. (See Luke 18:1). Spiritual strength comes from spiritual depth and fainting in prayer is showing sudden relapse, disability and other factors that paralyze the release of atomic power of prayer. Anything that takes strength to achieve cannot take weakness to attain. I am convicted in my heart that Jesus was giving away essential keys of how to invade spiritual spaces and realms by bringing down the overwhelming power of God in our lives. He was pointing to our human ignorance when it comes to praying with verifiable — authenticating results. Leaving the scene of an important life-altering meeting is canceling the appointment, which means that many people of God cancel their appointments with God because of lack of fervent — enduring prayers that will win the case.

Answered prayers are parts of the sustainability of the Christian life or it's just as empty as other religions. Finding a religion is opposing spiritual reality no matter how established the organization may be! It is written that "man shall not live by bread alone but by every word that proceeded out of the mouth of God." (See Matthew 4:). This is evident that a true relationship is not a matter of paperwork or computer simulations. There are things which are written as there are those things that the LORD

God is speaking even in the now. We have to understand that the material equivalencies cannot override the necessity for spiritual balance. For example, hearing Him speak has a different impact from reading about Him in every book in the world. If life itself is a love letter, the works of the cross would suffice the need for spiritual intimacy with the Holy Spirit, the glorified Christ and the Father. Prayer is seeking beyond all other forms of exhibitions as points of references to connect us with Him.

There must be a tremendous burden — excruciating thirst and hunger and deep passion in the heart of a man persisting and prostrating on the altar of prayer. It is the reason fasting is part of the birthing of spiritual maturity. Spiritual growth and maturity are measured by how much flesh has been shed off until it is completely put off to fully enter the spirit realms. Fasting and prayer are like the contact of fuel and fire! Where the connections between the Spirit and the natural man fail to ignite a spark, thirst and hunger for the outpouring must be used to draw the person closer. Spiritual deafness and blindness are not when the eyes are closed or when the ears are blocked; it's rather a spiritual phenomenon.

Proximity is determined by either closeness or distance, so fasting and prayer is closing the distance – bridging the gap to achieve the closeness with the LORD. The closeness is the secret to consummating spiritual intimacy with Him. Absent in the body is present with the LORD: the closer we are to Him, the greater distance we achieve away from the world and the demonic powers. Always, the consistency of spiritual closeness is achieved through fasting and prayer. Putting off the flesh can only be achieved in two ways: by physical death and personal surrender, submission and whole sacrifice. (See Hebrews 9:14). The perfect Will of God is received in the perfect state of spiritual positioning. Most importantly, the depth of spiritual problems and addictions is also countered from the depth of spiritual position. This is why there are besetting issues in peoples' lives that until they reach a certain spiritual threshold, the resolution of the matter will continue to remain on-hold. Besetting sins are controlling in nature; like retraction they draw our movements backward to hinder or stop our progress and momentum!

Often, people would say things like:

1. I have done everything but I cannot break free, so I am just going to let it be.
2. I don't really want to do this, but I cannot help myself.
3. I just can't find the answer so I am stock.

Our desires and actions are subject to change; however, many of us conclude that we are powerless — weak and tired, so we are unable to achieve our breakthrough.

You must never surrender your will to the enemy! If satan can control your thought life, he can control your life. Our soul and body can also be impacted. Our lives can be turned upside-down when we believe the deception and lies of the enemy. We will begin to think how could we ever break free from our captivity and bondage? We start to wonder if we will ever be able to regain the control of our lives again. When we move to take control of our physical craving desires, we can develop inner strength to rise above the controlling power.

Fasting and prayer is fighting for control of your life. By taking control of your eating habits, you are dedicating, committing and offering or sacrificing your life for the Will and purpose of God. When you fast, you are giving up necessary or enjoyable food as a demonstration and you are standing against the forces that have taken your spiritual and physical cravings or desires captive. The way to diminish the physical craving desires is by spiritual strength and not by might nor by power. (See Zechariah 4:6). The Bible said, I can do all things through Christ which strengthens me (Philippians 4:13). Many believers go to the LORD with the notion that He will do everything for them. However, every walk of freedom takes personal endurance. God will never do everything for us because there is a requirement for our decisive participation and engagement. He did not create us so that He would control us like robots. He gave us a free will to accept or reject Him. We either obey or disobey His Will and ignore His voice. He wants us to work out our salvation — go through the process to be made whole. He wants us to do our part of the work to realize our deliverance and freedom. The Bible said, Wherefore, my beloved, as ye have always obeyed, not as in my presence only, but now much more in my absence, work out your own salvation with fear and trembling (Philippians 2:12). Consistent fasting and prayers are the keys to breaking stubborn resistance, so you must learn to commit yourself continuously to fasting and praying until you achieve your breakthrough Jesus said, *this kind does not go out except by prayer and fasting* (Matthew 17:21). Sometimes, we pray and the answer is released immediately. Other times, we may have to remain asking, seeking and knocking until the answer is given to us. Discipline comes with great determination and expectations.

Important Steps to Take During Fasting and Prayers:

First step is to decide what type of fast and the length or how long the fast will last. If you are going to embark upon more frequent fasting, you will have to pen down the days you will fast. Once you are set with these arrangements, you must endeavor to accomplish the goal. To break free from spiritual captivity and bondage, we must follow all the strategies that the LORD God has directed us. Deeper roots can infiltrate and penetrate our subconscious and impact our emotions, mind and will — to affect our desires and behaviors.

The Bible said, *For though we walk in the flesh, we do not war after the flesh: (For the weapons of our warfare are not carnal, but mighty through God to the pulling down of strong holds;) Casting down imaginations, and every high thing that exalteth itself against the knowledge of God, and bringing into captivity every thought to the obedience of Christ; And having in a readiness to revenge all disobedience, when your obedience is fulfilled* (2 Corinthians 10:3-6).

We Must Denounce and Renounce All False Influences and Controls:

We must have the ability to know the false and the counterfeit. You need discernment of spirits, the inspiration of the Spirit and the revelation of God. Many people will be victimized and exploited in the end-times as they err from the truth. They will accept the counterfeit and expose themselves to the false.

The Bible said, *But I fear, lest by any means, as the serpent beguiled Eve through his subtilty, so your minds should be corrupted from the simplicity that is in Christ* (2 Corinthians 11:3).

There are many counterfeiters today and we are faced with great falsehood. Darkness is covering the world and gross darkness is covering the people. Errors are everywhere and people are deceiving and being deceived. The choices of books, movies, music and websites we visit can easily entangle our lives. People are consciously and unconsciously opening their lives to the occult, New Age, black and white magic as well as different other false religions. John 10:10a said, *the thief cometh not, but for to steal, and to kill, and to destroy.*

We Must Deal with All Deception and Lies: Both self and outside deception share a common outcome. We are simply deceived and we need the truth. The truth is very important to receive our deliverance and freedom.

Psalms 51:6 said, *Behold, thou desirest truth in the inward parts: and in the hidden part You shalt make me to know wisdom.*

Some of the ways we fall into deception are:
We deceive ourselves when we hear the Word of the LORD God and fail to live by or do the Word:

And he answered and said unto them, my Mother and my brethren are these which hear the word of God, and do it (Luke 8:21).

But be ye doers of the word, and not hearers only, deceiving your own selves (James 1:22).

Therefore, to him that knows to do good, and doeth it not, to him it is sin (James 4:17).

We deceive ourselves when we hide, cover or deny our sins:

He that covers his sins shall not prosper: but whoso confesses and forsakes them shall have mercy (Proverbs 28:13).

If we say that we have no sin, we deceive ourselves, and the truth is not in us. If we confess our sins, he is faithful and just to forgive us our sins, and to cleanse us from all unrighteousness. If we say that we have not sinned, we make him a liar, and his word is not in us (1 John 1:8-10).

We deceive ourselves when we wrongly estimate and appreciate our valuable worth, exalt ourselves and make ourselves who we are not:

And whosoever shall exalt himself shall be abased; and he that shall humble himself shall be exalted (Matthew 23:12).

For if a man think himself to be something, when he is nothing, he deceiveth himself (Galatians 6:3).

We deceive ourselves when we use the world as our measuring standards: When we evaluate and estimate ourselves by the standards of the world instead of the LORD God, we fall into deception and lies of the enemy:

The Bible said, *let no man deceive himself. If any man among you seems to be wise in this world, let him become a fool, that he may be wise. For the wisdom of this world is foolishness with God. For it is written, He taketh the wise in their own craftiness* (1 Corinthians 3:18-19).

We deceive ourselves when we think that we can escape from the consequences of our sins. Always, deception and bondage go together:

The Bible said, *and ye shall know the truth, and the truth shall make you free* (John 8:32).

Know ye not that the unrighteous shall not inherit the kingdom of God? Be not deceived: neither fornicators, nor idolaters, nor adulterers, nor effeminate, nor abusers of themselves with mankind, nor thieves, nor covetous, nor drunkards, nor revilers, nor extortioners, shall inherit the kingdom of God. And such were some of you: but ye are washed, but ye are sanctified, but ye are justified in the name of the Lord Jesus, and by the Spirit of our God (1 Corinthians 6:9-11).

We Must Forgive Others: When we choose not to forgive others, we put ourselves in spiritual bondage to them and to sin. Forgiveness is a personal decision; however, we need the help of the Holy Spirit to truly forgive others after they have wronged us. The LORD requires us to forgive others; therefore, forgiveness is mandatory in our Christian life. When we forgive others, we also experience God's forgiveness in our own lives. True forgiveness is a remedial prescription and cure.

Apostle Paul wrote: *To whom ye forgive anything, I forgive also: for if I forgave anything, to whom I forgave it, for your sakes forgave I it in the person of Christ; Lest Satan should get an advantage of us: for we are not ignorant of his devices* (2 Corinthians 2:10-11).

You Must Submit to God's Authority: Submitting to God's authority and placing yourself under those whom He has raised up to lead you is part of the keys to dealing with personal rebellion. Authority and power always respect authority and power because it understands authority and power. Please see the case of the centurion (Matthew 8:8-10). We are subjected to different chains of authority and power that the LORD God has appointed over us.

We are biblically commanded to submit to:

To the LORD God: *We have sinned, and have committed iniquity, and have done wickedly, and have rebelled, even by departing from thy precepts and from thy judgments: To the Lord our God belong mercies and forgivenesses, though we have rebelled against him* (Daniel 9:5, 9).

Civil Governments: *Let every soul be subject unto the higher powers. For there is no power but of God: the powers that be are ordained of God. Whosoever therefore resisteth the power, resisteth the ordinance of God: and they that resist shall receive to themselves damnation. For rulers are not a terror to good works, but to the evil. Wilt thou then not be afraid of the power? do that which is good, and thou shalt have praise of the same: For he is the minister of God to thee for good. But if thou do that which is evil, be afraid; for he beareth not the sword in vain: for he is the minister of God, a revenger to execute wrath upon him that doeth evil. Wherefore ye must needs be subject, not only for wrath, but also for conscience sake. For for this cause pay ye tribute also: for they are God's ministers, attending continually upon this very thing. Render therefore to all their dues: tribute to whom tribute is due; custom to whom custom; fear to whom fear; honour to whom honour* (Romans 13:1-7).

Our Church Leadership: *Obey them that have the rule over you, and submit yourselves: for they watch for your souls, as they that must give account, that they may do it with joy,* *and not with grief: for that is unprofitable for you* (Hebrews 13:17).

Our Parents: *Children, obey your parents in the Lord: for this is right. Honour thy father and mother; (which is the first commandment with promise;) That it may be well with thee, and thou mayest live long on the earth* (Ephesians 6:1-3).

Our Employers: *Submit yourselves to every ordinance of man for the Lord's sake: whether it be to the king, as supreme; Or unto governors, as unto them that are sent by him for the punishment of evildoers, and for the praise of them that do well. For so is the will of God, that with well doing ye may put to silence the ignorance of foolish men: As free, and not using your liberty for a cloke of maliciousness, but as the servants of God. Honour all men. Love the brotherhood. Fear God. Honour the king. Servants, be subject to your masters with all fear; not only to the good and gentle, but also to the froward. For this is thankworthy, if a man for conscience toward God endure grief, suffering wrongfully* (1 Peter 2:13-19).

Our Husbands: *Likewise, ye wives, be in subjection to your own husbands; that, if any obey not the word, they also may without the word be won by the conversation of the wives; While they behold your chaste conversation coupled with fear. Whose adorning let it not be that outward adorning of plaiting the hair, and of wearing of gold, or of putting on of apparel; But let it be the hidden man of the heart, in*

that which is not corruptible, even the ornament of a meek
and quiet spirit, which is in the sight of God of great price (1
Peter 3:1-4).

We are personally responsible for the things we do
even if we are coerced, tempted, or deceived by others.
Therefore, we must endeavor to take appropriate steps to
remedy the situations before we can begin to realize normalcy in our lives. Pride is enemy of personal responsibility. We must accept the responsibility for our situations.
Pride and self-exaltation can lead to captivity and bondage. If the Son therefore shall make you free, ye shall be
free indeed (John 8:36); however, freedom is never passive. There are works on the part of the Savior as well as
those being saved. Wherefore, my beloved, as ye have always obeyed, not as in my presence only, but now much
more in my absence, work out your own salvation with
fear and trembling (Philippians 2:12). Surrendering and
submitting to Jesus Christ and the Holy Spirit are active
engagements, and we can exercise our free-will to obey
or disobey the law and voice of the LORD God. Always,
the confession of our sins is mandatory. If we say that we
have no sin, we deceive ourselves, and the truth is not in
us. If we confess our sins, he is faithful and just to forgive us our sins, and to cleanse us from all unrighteousness (1 John 1:8-9). Sometimes, we mistake repentance
for a pause. However, admitting our wrong is taking full
responsibility instead of passing the blame to others. (See

Genesis 3:12-13). Some people think that repentance is formality: they repeatedly confess their sins, but immediately turn back to the same behaviors. Often, the reason is because of bondage. Addiction is part of bondage as sin is part of addiction. Sin leads to captivity and bondage in the lives of the people of God. The formalities of repentance can only lead to more excuses or tolerance for the same behaviors.

The Bible said, *neither yield ye your members as instruments of unrighteousness unto sin: but yield yourselves unto God, as those that are alive from the dead, and your members as instruments of righteousness unto God* (Romans 6:13).

Responsibility is part of humility; therefore, when we take responsibility for our sins, we humble ourselves before the LORD to secure the release and freedom we desire. Disassociation is vital component of true repentance because evil communication corrupts good manner. Some friends and acquaintances are snares on your path of life. Every individual is predisposed to certain behavioral characteristics, often emanating from different sources.

They could be related but not limited to:

1. Emotional/mental or psychological issues
2. Genetics/background or foundational problems
3. Sin, trespass, iniquity and transgression

4. People we follow or those who have influence over our lives
5. Satanic or demonic activities

We must reject all participation with the sins of other people and their influences over our lives including family history. (See Exodus 20:4-5; Gal. 5:24). Bible promises are fundamental in possessing our personal inheritance, so we must acknowledge the written records and prayerfully ask for the release of the blessings. Scriptures are fulfilled through fasting and prayers — the Holy Spirit moves to bring those things to reality in our lives.

These Scriptures will help you in your prayers:

For ye are bought with a price: therefore, glorify God in your body, and in your spirit, which are God's (1 Corinthians 6:20).

And they that are Christ's have crucified the flesh with the affections and lusts (Galatians 5:24).

But God, who is rich in mercy, for his great love wherewith he loved us, even when we were dead in sins, hath quickened us together with Christ, (by grace ye are saved;) And hath raised us up together, and made us sit together in heavenly places in Christ Jesus (Ephesians 2:4-6).

But if we walk in the light, as he is in the light, we have fellowship one with another, and the blood of Jesus Christ his Son cleanseth us from all sin (1 John 1:7).

Here are some key points to remember:

1. Renunciation and denunciation.
2. Acknowledgment and repentance of all your sins, transgressions, iniquities, trespasses, offenses and faults.
3. Forgiveness of others who have wronged you and praying for them.
4. Surrender yourself and submit to the guidance of the Holy Spirit.
5. Separate yourself from the company of evil and wicked people.

Responsibility is taking important steps to address critical issues in your life. Fasting and prayer are part of engaging in spiritual warfare against the enemy, and it is why you face additional challenges when you attempt to fast. The Bible said, *howbeit this kind goes not out but by prayer and fasting* (Matthew 17:21). In spiritual warfare, you must exercise diligent caution to utilize all available weapons to defeat your enemy. Warfare always take strategic approach including designed plans! Please see Isaiah 58:1-14.

Because he hath set his love upon me, therefore will I deliver him: I will set him on high, because he hath known my name. He shall call upon me, and I will answer him: I will be with him in trouble; I will deliver him, and honour him. With long life will I satisfy him, and shew him my salvation (Psalms 91:14-16).

Chapter Eight

SUCCESSFULLY
SINGLE

In this Chapter, I want to focus on empowering, equipping and edifying every single woman, who is on a journey to experience wholeness. I want to communicate relevant truth: to teach, inspire and reveal, and to help and encourage you wherever you are. I want you to see that there is more than what meets the eye.

And the LORD God said, it is not good that man should be alone; I will make him a help meet for him (Genesis 2:18).

Becoming a Kingdom Single in the 21st century is extremely challenging due to enormous amount of temptation in the media and society as a whole. We have so much peer pressures today! What you must know is that everything is achievable by the grace of God. The LORD is ever present to help you live an optimal Christian lifestyle regardless of what is happening around you. Emphatically speaking, you can be successfully single while waiting for a life's partner!

The Bible said, *it is not by might, nor by your power, but by my Spirit saith the LORD* (Zechariah 4:6).

Some women have learned to seek and receive roses, dinners, diamonds, pearls, minx coats, jewelry and companionship and yet, they never have the stability, security, and satisfaction of true identity and real love they desire or crave for in life.

Many single women desire to find "Mr. Right." Most of them do not realize that they were not designed or purposed to search for Mr. Right to begin with. They were designed to walk in their Kingdom purpose and destiny.

Women are unique and peculiar created works of God. They are the products of the Living God and the idea of the Creator. God had women in His thought from the very beginning.

Throughout my ministry tenure, I constantly hear women lowering their standards just to have men in their lives, so they will feel complete and whole. There are many women who succumb to all kinds of abuses because of low self-esteem and desperation for companionship. They have pressing needs to feel loved and desired, but instead they are bruised, battered, scared and broken. Some women have become damaged goods.

Why do some women feel lost without men in their lives? I remember the incident with the woman at the well. In John Chapter 4, Jesus had a divine appointment with this thirsty woman. She was not only physically thirsty; Jesus knew she was spiritually dehydrated. Jesus revealed that she was not married, but had been with five different men.

Usually, the women with the greatest mess in their lives, have the greatest potential within. What they need is for their potentials to be awakened. The Samaritan woman as she is known, had enormous problems -- jumping from man to man, trying to fill the void that only Jesus Christ Himself could satisfy in her life!

Jesus specifically went on a mission and waited for her at the well. Sounds like a divine set up and appointment to me. He was there waiting on a thirsty woman, as the Living Water that satisfies all those who are thirsty! Jesus Christ was everything that the woman at the well will ever need and that one encounter with the Master, changed the trajectory of her life from that moment onward. The LORD was strategic in approaching her, because as a prophet He knew she would go and broadcast that she had met a man who told her everything about her life. (See John Chapter 4).

Today, I see tears flowing from women of all ages as I counsel them. It does not matter the specific issue; the same theme seemed to occur or repeat in their lives.

The deception and lies of the enemy have caused many women to become desperate. Where purpose is unknown, abuse is always inevitable. It is my endeavor to bring back into the heart and mind of every woman whether young or old the true beauty and essence of being a woman. I want you to know that you are not only a woman, but a woman of purpose, power and distinction! Your uniqueness is part of divine order!

If you can only think like the woman that the LORD God created you to be, your relationship will not only come into proper perspective, your entire life will take on a brand-new meaning. The shift will begin to cause the formation of spiritual alignment that will revolutionize your physical existence. Application of Life is trans-positional, so a spiritual shift can alter the physical environment and atmosphere. The same applies to who you are!

Some singles fail to realize the beauty of singlehood. In some cultures, it is a disgrace to remain single at a certain age. There is a pressured demand to find a mate. Nevertheless, I want to make it absolutely clear that you must learn to embrace the season and beauty of singlehood. During the period of singlehood, it is imperative that you take some time to discover who you are, and what you are placed in this earth to do, instead of looking and searching for love in all the wrong places. So many women are distracted in life because they are looking for a person to complete them. Dear sister and daughter of Zion, the only person who can complete you is your Creator. The void that is in your heart and soul was placed there by your Creator Himself and only He can fill the vacuum and affirm your identity, worth and value.

Many women are placing their lives on hold while searching for their life's partner and getting themselves entangled and stuck. It is said that "the worst thing outside of hell fire is a bad marriage." Very often, people choose to ignore the fact. The question is, why not use this precious time to perfect your life, skills and God given abilities while waiting on your life's partner?

As we venture further, I want you to carefully examine Proverbs 4:23, the Bible said, to guard and pay close attention to protect your heart -- watch your heart with a sense of urgency to safeguard it.

There are two components to guarding something: 1) is to prevent it from escape and 2), is to control the passageway. We are personally responsible to guard our lives from relationships and anything that might deteriorate and damage us.

God wants you to be a whole woman before you enter into a marriage relationship. You must understand that "wholeness" here is not because of marriage. The LORD is the one that makes you whole in Him! He wants you to know your identity or who you are. You are a daughter of a Royal Kingdom! When you are not whole, your life will always attract those who will undermine, devalue and mistreat you! It takes value to understand value. It takes worth to estimate and appreciate worth! Value and worth attract the same! It is the law of commonality!

A half of woman will always be attracted to a half of man and vice versa. In fact, some women are single because God is trying to heal and restore their lives to embrace their purpose and destiny. When your life is not whole, you will continue to attract something that will ultimately hurt your life. Abuse and mistreatment work like the laws of gravity. When you think you are going up, you are on your way down!

Single women must not see themselves as needy and desperate! What they need is to learn how to celebrate and appreciate themselves on their road to wholeness. It is not good to grow up thinking that the pinnacle of success is having someone in your life. I want you to begin to adopt the right mindset towards your season of singlehood and soon, you will never starve for an emotional connection again. You will no longer be an average single, but a sophisticated and exceptional single!

God desires for you to seek after Him and not a after a man. He knows what He wants for your life. He wants you to have an unusual encounter with Him that will change and transform your whole life. God has given women massive influence; therefore, women are extremely powerful, skillful and creative. We must harness the power and channel it in the right direction.

Jeremiah, the Great Prophet, called for the wailing women to come and let them take up a wailing. The Prophet of God was looking for women who knew how to pray – He was calling for intercessors and prayer warriors! He wants them to take up and occupy their spiritual posts and mourn. Women can affect so much change through prayers! They can shift and move nations or Kingdoms into divine order.

A praying woman is God's intelligent agent in the Earth realm. God does not give women spiritual blessings to keep them to themselves! They are gifted to edify others! They are gifted to enrich His kingdom! They are empowered to accomplish His great purposes for their lives. I demand that you commit and submit your talents, gifts, dreams, visions and desires to the LORD God today, and you will begin to see His divine establishment in your life.

In some cultures, the women are perceived as personal properties, objects of sexual gratification, domestic slaves, personal servants, unintelligent creatures, weak and worthy of abuse and humiliation. Only spiritually intelligent men are able to recognize the strength, resilience, worth and value of women today. A woman multiplies and enlarges what is given to her. If you have an idea, she will give you a business plan. If you give her a house, she will make it a home. If you give her a seed, she will give you a child. She is a fruit-bearing seed – a help meet according to divine allocation! A vessel designed for the master's use!

Women, being single is not a death sentence! You are not a death-row inmate!

As godly women, we can be relevant by being examples to our daughters and the younger generation! The Bible holds us responsible and accountable as mothers. Some women are producing an ungodly generation today. Our children are our fruits! We can destroy the power of curses; however, we must be prepared to change certain behavior patterns.

Christian godly Mothers have great responsibilities to undertake. We must not raise up strange daughters! We must dare to stand upright in this dark age. We must be the light to many, and influence with the right spirit to raise up a generation of royal daughters for our majestic King! You can be a minority with a grand purpose in life. We must teach our daughters that they are more than their bodies; that they are fearfully and wonderfully made. You have to see why you do not have to give up your body for illicit sexual behaviors to feel significant because you are priceless. You are not just your breasts, butt, hips, and thighs! In fact, you have a brain and intelligence besides the Spirit of God inside of you. God has given you creative abilities to transform the world around you.

Listen to me Single Woman, you do not need to adopt the spirit of the land, which promotes sexiness. The culture dictates that you must be revealing to be relevant and accepted. However, it is a lie! I understand that we live in this world, but we are not of this world. You must not allow the dictations of the flesh to rule over your life: you will become the slave of your fleshly appetites. You can either control the flesh or it will control you! Control is part of rulership and subjection! God has provided the power to control your emotions, mind and will. God has given you the ability to control your sexual appetite. You must be extremely decisive in your resistance. You must be very determined to pursue after the LORD God! He will deliver you from seeking for attention in all the wrong ways and places.

Dear precious daughters, a man is never going to "see your worth and value" just because you share a sexual contact with him. For a man, physical intimacy does not equal to a relationship! You must understand that sleeping together sexually and having a relationship are two different things entirely!

You must cease from giving yourself away – refrain from sleeping with men because you desire their love and affection or approval. A man is not the final judge of your worth and value as a woman. You must take back your sense of morality and self-respect! You must safeguard your purity as a treasured item. Christ-likeness and womanhood are synonymous. This is why the older women were charged to teach the younger women about important godly principles and what it truly means to live for and serve the LORD.

The Bible declares, *the unmarried woman cares for the things of the LORD, that she may be holy in body and spirit* (1 Corinthians 7:34b).

This Scripture did not say that the unmarried woman was lazy and depressed, but rather she was busy minding the things of the LORD and preserving or keeping herself pure. A kingdom single will embrace her assignment with grace whether at home, in the community, a workplace or the Church.

Singleness is equivalent to wholeness – to be unbroken and undivided. Women are relevant in more ways than one. They are relevant to the society. They are life-givers, community leaders, advocates and activists. They are vital asset! They are full of potential! They are strong and capable! They can wage good warfare: on behalf of their families, communities, cities, states and nations or kingdoms. They can impact their regions on their knees and with their resources for the LORD. Women have special equipping of the LORD to do battles in the realms of the spirit.

Satan understands that women will fight for their families, just as the lioness guards her territory and defend against dangers. The devil hates some women because they possess the spirit of the overcomer on the inside. *And I will put enmity between thee and the woman, and between thy seed and her seed; it shall bruise thy head, and thou shalt bruise his heel* (Genesis 3:15). God has released peculiar weapons to His daughters around the world to wage wars. He is showing them the secret plans of the enemy against the human race in the end-times!

Satan sets generational curses in motion to impact people's lives from early childhood, to hinder them from birth and stop them from walking in their greatness. The plan of the enemy is always to steal, and to kill, and to destroy even from infant or embryonic stages. (See Matthew 2:1-18). He uses weapons like rejection, low self-esteem, distrust, rape and molestation besides other forms of abuses to strike their victims. He desires to turn people's lives into damaged goods and ruined lives, so they will not rise up to become threats to his kingdom.

Jesus came that you might have life, and that you might have it more abundantly (John 10:10b). Satan does not want the women to be made whole because a whole woman is too dangerous for the kingdom of darkness. Wholeness is attributes of dominion as we see with Adam in the Garden of Eden. (See Genesis 1:26)!

The enemy wants to destroy! He wants to decapitate! He wants to beat, bruise, abuse and batter. He sends the wrong people in your life. He assigns agents of darkness on your pathway to ruin your life. He wants you to walk in bitterness, and carry around hurts for years. He does not want you to obtain healing and restoration that Jesus Christ died on the cross to give you!

I say therefore to the unmarried and widows, It is good for them if they abide even as I. But if they cannot contain, let them marry: for it is better to marry than to burn (1 Corinthians 7:8-9).

Chapter Nine

BEFORE YOU SAY, "I DO"

M arriage is part of the fulfillment of the spiritual order of life between two genders — a man and woman. They come together in a marital union to raise a family, a household, and a home. Nevertheless, to commit to a marriage relationship, it is extremely important to know the history or backgrounds of the participants. Many people indulge because of physical attractions, affections and personal possessions. In the earlier days, before entering into a marriage, the lineages are vetted including checking the families whether they relate to good or evil things.

Be ye not unequally yoked together with unbelievers: for what fellowship hath righteousness with unrighteousness? and what communion hath light with darkness? (2 Corinthians 6:14).

There are several questions that must be asked and carefully evaluated before venturing into a marriage commitment. Marrying a person, you do not know his or her identity or lifestyle can open your life to painful future experiences. Your marriage arrangements may look beautiful at the beginning but things can easily turn bitter down the stretch. The history of the family you are marrying into can become part of your experiences in life. The compounding of your battles may prove unbearable, and the marriage might fail under great pressures. A good marriage begins with careful vetting and its why background checks and security clearances are necessary. Foundational problems are the more damaging challenges in marriages because people have no clues about investing into spiritual knowledge when it comes to marriages. Lineages — biological and genealogical traces are parts of record-keeping and revisiting these archives can yield important key solutions in marriages.

Now these are the generations of Terah: Terah begat Abram, Nahor, and Haran; and Haran begat Lot. And Haran died before his father Terah in the land of his nativity, in Ur of the Chaldees. And Abram and Nahor took them wives: the name of Abram's wife was Sarai; and the name of Nahor's wife, Milcah, the daughter of Haran, the father of Milcah, and the father of Iscah (Genesis 11:27-29).

Many family problems — spiritually and physically constitutes tremendous hindrance to the household progress. There are families that struggle to marry and there are those who go through difficult hardship to achieve prosperity and great things in life. Some families experience setbacks and disappointments or breakdown at the edge of marriages. There are also families that suffer reoccurring attacks of different sicknesses and diseases and some families cannot keep and maintain employment.

You must carefully ask these important questions including many other questions to help you in your marital decision-making process:

- What are the common sinful behaviors in the family background?
- What are the common sicknesses and diseases that run in the family line?
- What are most common problems in the family?
- If the parents are deceased, what were the causes of deaths?
- Are the parents married, separated, or divorced?
- What type of work do the parents do?
- What religions do the parents practice?
- What are the problems that challenged the parents in their marriage?
- Do you have a strong relationship with your parents as well as the extended family?
- What are the noticeable traits or behaviors of your parents?
- Have your parents at any time pronounced curses upon your life?

- Do you dream about your deceased parents often?
- Have your parents ever regretted conceiving and given birth to you?
- What do you know about your grandparents and great grandparents?
- What is your private lifestyle like?
- What did your parent(s) worship: idols, false religions, occultism, nature, ancestors or other things?
- Are these things currently being worshiped or practiced in your family?
- What are the common problems with the firstborn, first daughter, and last born as well as other siblings in the family?
- Does the family have love and unity among them?
- Are their sudden failures at the edge of success in the family?
- Do you have a nickname, a traditional name, and title: what are their meanings?
- Does the family have a pattern of hardship and poverty?
- Is there a set time that anyone in the family realized some type of a breakthrough?
- Are there sudden or untimely deaths and what is the average lifespan in the family?
- Has the family experienced high rate of separation and divorce both in the past and present?

Marriage has so many unique characteristics that re-quires exhaustive investigation to unravel. The mysteries behind marriage is more than scientific; therefore, en-tering into a marriage relationship is embracing real life events beyond finding a beautiful woman or handsome man to entangle with. In fact, before the vow of marriage, there are extended intelligence efforts that must be con-ducted on both parties. The order of marriage calls for biological and genealogical inquires similar to background checks and security clearances. One is looking into the other's history. It is important to understand the spiritual and physical implications of marriage. There is a spiritual aspect of marriage even as the soul and body are impacted, not only in times of sexual contact but also other parts of life. I want us to look at the first perfect marriage involv-ing the first man and woman. In Genesis 1:26 we found,

And God said, let us make man in our image, after our likeness (Genesis 1:26a).

Sometimes we question, why do certain cultures have to look into the family history of the bride and groom? We feel that it is unnecessary, and if two people find love, they should just proceed to do whatever they want. This is precarious because the vetting process is the key to hid-den discoveries. Like children go through paternity test to establish the parental backgrounds, marriage on the other hand must take beyond physical assessment: beauty-check, sexual performance, attraction and affection, or social status. Because the order of marriage involves finding the right wife among many men and women, the challenge would be how to begin. Boyfriend and girlfriend scenarios only create additional violation and the reason is that starting on the wrong foot does not mean you could easily make the changes. There is no way to separate marriage from careful spiritual investigation. Without tracing the biological and genealogical history, it will be hard to establish the family spiritually and physically.

With the first marriage, we can easily read, *And the LORD God said, it is not good that the man should be alone; I will make him a help meet for him* (Genesis 2:18).

And the LORD God caused a deep sleep to fall upon Adam, and he slept: and he took one of his ribs, and closed up the flesh instead thereof; And the rib, which the LORD God had taken from man, made he a woman, and brought her unto the man. And Adam said, this is now bone of my bones, and flesh of my flesh: she shall be called Woman, because she was taken out of Man. Therefore, shall a man leave his father and his mother, and shall cleave unto his wife: and they shall be one flesh (Genesis 2:21-24).

We see the woman taken out of the man, and united with the man. The Bible said, *what God had joined together*, so the first marriage was joined by God. The making process is so important in establishing the order of life because where there is no history, it's extremely challenging to investigate people's backgrounds. Why is it necessary to know people's backgrounds in marital commitments? For two people to walk together, they must agree and for two to become one, they must share the same makeup. Examining the makeup is looking deep into the components to verify the compatibility. Therefore, besides asking to know about the families of marriage partners, prayers are vital ingredients to bring the Author of marriage into the equation.

Because marriage touches the fabrics of the whole person, we must look into the spirit, we must look into the emotion, mind and will, we must look at the body, and we must look into the bloodlines, the family trees and other areas of their lives, etc. The things that run in the families are hereditary — there are transfers as there are inheritances both spiritual and physical. When two become one, they compound whatever they brought into the union from their respective family heritages including upbringing, traditions, customs and behavioral characteristics. The same applies to all spiritual activities: witchcraft, occultism, idolatry, immorality, addictions, proclivities, dysfunctions, poverty, curses and many other negative issues. The unexpected consequences are what we are endeavoring to resolve before they explode to destroy the marriage prematurely. Inheritances are not a matter of pick-and-chose because they are delivered like clusters of packages: the things that pertain to life are released into our lives and the material things are delivered separately. This is to say that some of the things happening in people's lives are traceable from their family lineages. They are contracted like infections and transmitted diseases and spread across the family trees to yield the same fruits.

You must see marriage as a lifetime investment and not a periodic contractual agreement that is subject to certain terms and conditions. Therefore, it is worth all the efforts to search relentlessly to uncover the traps of the enemy. Some agendas of the evil one is hidden — concealed beneath the surface and they are suddenly set off like a time-bomb. Many marriages are left ruined or utterly destroyed by unsuspecting diabolical enemy plots. Exposing the enemy plans are the keys to resolving them before they go into effect and begin to wreak havoc on your relationships. Preparedness is greater than ignorance and negligence: you must protect what you value by adding more value and protection around it to prevent a sudden deterioration and eventual collapse.

Marriage is a spiritual bedrock in a human life although people lack the awareness of the severity of the negative consequences of entering into a wrongful marriage agreement. The impact can traumatize your life for years and therapy or counseling may prove ineffective. Demonic roots in a marriage takes more than psychological evaluations and medical recommendations to cure. Spiritual things are spiritually diagnosed — discerned, investigated and carefully estimated, and the cure requires spiritual medication of the word, authority and power of God. Preventive measures are parts of the acceleration of life because the time it would take to find a new remedy could prove fatal for many. The same applies to marriage relationships. The investment we make when it comes to marital commitments will yield the fruit later, so our beginning is crucial in safeguarding the future of our hardworks. There are so many factors that can coerce a marriage commitment and the vow of marriage as well as the marriage ceremonies are only the physical parts. Marriage is a lifetime work and when we stop working, the marriage will cease to work. Breaking-up and breaking-down shows a point of disconnection that all known efforts to save our works have failed, and this is why some people will feel like failures.

Before you say, "I do," take the oath or vow to enter into a marriage relationship, there are lists of what to do — beginning with spiritual intelligence to investigating both family backgrounds. The records are vital to the success and longevity of the life of the marriage union. The valves or cords linking the bloodlines are similar to life-support systems and like blood transfusions, everything flow through the pipelines of the family trees. We have to shut off the valves and cut the cords, break the ties, detach ourselves until there are no more connections and contacts   spiritually and physically. The Bible said, *neither give place to the devil* (Ephesians 4:27).

Here are some extremely important areas to focus on:

1) You must not give the enemy any room in your marriage venture by opening the doors through sexual contacts before the oath of marriage vows:

The enemy is looking to become part of your life: sexual sin is within the body and the parts of the body used for sexual contacts can become dedicated or offered to the enemy. The future battles to deliver these body parts can add great frustration into your marriage life. There is spiritual harvest of organs: when the organs are infested by demonic plagues — sicknesses and diseases and no medical procedures can cure it, the demons holding the organs may be placing a demand to reject the medical procedures. Physically, some organs may have to be cut off. Organ harvests are practiced spiritually and physically, and many people do not know that demons can take away people's limbs as well as killing and destroying their lives. This is part of stealing, killing and destroying! Lust demons and spirits of perversion have no respect for marriage because lust and perversion are not element of love.

Although you may feel some attraction and gravitate affectionately toward the other person, the response may be careless and lead to a long-time entrapment. Spirit husbands, wives, boyfriends, and girlfriends exercise certain rights in people's lives. There claims and counterclaims are not fabrications, so it's not a matter of ignoring their accusations. Rights also confer legitimate authority and power, when the authority and power are executed, you must go through the legal processes to reclaim and recover what belongs to you. Sexual contact is a consummation of a lawful marriage and when the contact is exercised wrongfully, it will become either fornication or adultery and the enemy will move to attach himself to the relationship.

There are different ways that people experience deliverance including vindication from false accusations and legal misrepresentations. Many people destroy their love lives even before they ever grow to reach the threshold of marriage commitments. They sacrifice their life through illegal sex trade and demons will rush all over their lives to fight every relationship they enter into. When the enemy claims marital status with you, it means that an open door was created through illicit behaviors — whether through lust, perversion, or other sexual avenues. Sex is not only a physical contact because looking at a man or woman with lustful and perverse sexual desires register in the spirit realms as engaging in intercourse. The heart and the soul can connect without our physical body coming into proximity. Our lives are built like folders and sub-folders and whatever are saved in those compartments cannot be easily deleted, so the proofs are ever present unless we repent before the LORD. Demons will not voluntarily give up their rights until their rights are taken away. This why people fight relentlessly to be delivered from demonic powers. It is not because the demons are so powerful and unstoppable but because of certain rights and the process to address them. Marriage is honorable in all, and the bed undefiled: but whoremongers and adulterers God will judge (Hebrews 13:4).

2) From a spiritual and physical legal standpoint, it is imperative to conduct thorough search into the life of your partner before committing to marriage:

The search is not merely to intrude or implicate your partner through your fact-finding but to alleviate, reconcile and resolve all outstanding spiritual and physical implications. Matters of privacy are important; however, without addressing certain issues in the marriage, there will be no privacy in the future. Demons do not support human privacy; in fact, they expose and openly embarrass people to undermine their intelligence and degrade their lives and values. Joining two together and unifying them as one is compounding all aspects of their lives. The law of inheritance is triggered by different other laws because of the unique applications. Unanswered accusations can lead to endless legal complications. You may not realize it in the beginning until somewhere down the line. The same way that certain information obtained through the cause of legal preceding must be carefully preserved and used only for that matter, using them for personal black-mail can open the door for attacks on the family. When two become one, both share all the implications as well as consequences. What people don't often understand is that neither the wife nor the husband is better than the other. They must work together to save, defend and protect each other or incriminate themselves.

And the man said, the woman whom thou gavest to be with me, she gave me of the tree, and I did eat. And the LORD God said unto the woman, what is this that thou hast done? And the woman said, the serpent beguiled me, and I did eat. And the LORD God said unto the serpent, Because thou hast done this, thou art cursed above all cattle, and above every beast of the field; upon thy belly shalt thou go, and dust shalt thou eat all the days of thy life: And I will put enmity between thee and the woman, and between thy seed and her seed; it shall bruise thy head, and thou shalt bruise his heel. Unto the woman he said, I will greatly multiply thy sorrow and thy conception; in sorrow thou shalt bring forth children; and thy desire shall be to thy husband, and he shall rule over thee. And unto Adam he said, Because thou hast hearkened unto the voice of thy wife, and hast eaten of the tree, of which I commanded thee, saying, Thou shalt not eat of it: cursed is the ground for thy

*sake; in sorrow shalt thou eat of it all the days of thy life;
Thorns also and thistles shall it bring forth to thee; and thou
shalt eat the herb of the field; In the sweat of thy face shalt
thou eat bread, till thou return unto the ground; for out of it
was thou taken: for dust thou art, and unto dust* (See Genesis 3:12-19).

Proper authority and power must know that legal docu-
ments are never for personal use. This is why they are
preserved with integrity so they will not be contaminated.
Contaminated evidence cannot be admitted in the court
of law because justice must be rendered justly and righ-
teously. Looking into your partner's history is rightly au-
thorized by God; however, any time we misuse it, other
important issues will be furthermore protected and secured – kept away from any access or intrusion. A judge
cannot freely share the information of an accused pub-
licly unless there is a need for such transparency. Some
partners spend enormous time accusing each or other and
bringing up one other's pasts without knowing that they
are partakers by inheritance.

The woman is the glory of the man or defensive covering and the man is the head of the woman — both the
prayers of the wife and husband sanctify either partner.
Washing the woman with the word is not exposing her
past. Exposing your husband is not defending him. The
enemy uses legal implications and complications to bury

families in legal quagmire. This is what hinders the blessings because God is a righteous and just Judge. Helping each other break free is better than destroying each other's life. Some marriages are disasters today: they are marriages made in hell. The enemy has infiltrated and penetrated the foundation to pollute the fabrics of the relationship. Marriage is sacred and the preservation must take adequate engagement — covering both spiritual and physical aspects or it will begin to fall apart! And I heard a loud voice saying in heaven, Now is come salvation, and strength, and the kingdom of our God, and the power of his Christ: for the accuser of our brethren is cast down, **which accused them before our God day and night** (Revelation 12:10).

3) Confess your faults and offenses one to another and pray for one another:

Personal disputes are not court matters. They can be resolved privately between the partners — husband and wife. We have to see that prayer — petition and request are legal terminology. All prayers are prayed according to legal terms and conditions and likewise, all answers to prayers are obtained legally. Admitting your faults one to another will set the stage for remediation so there will be no further provocation and escalation. Always, accusing your partner helps the enemy built a case against the marriage and family. Remember that the word of God has set the perimeters around marriage conducts and behaviors, and violating these legal orders allows the adversary to step in. Altercations can be fueled by the enemy to boost the negative outcome of the battle or family warfare. Accepting blame for doing wrong and apologizing to one another can keep the enemy from your personal business. If you have to resolve your family dispute in the court of law, you are not only immature, but you must prepare yourself for even more legal problems in the court of accusations. The enemy accuses you day and night, so he is not missing any opportunity. He is looking into your life in every way including your marriage life to sabotage your marital vows and commitment. He is a thief, a killer, and a destroyer, and you must learn to keep your marriage away from him and his Kingdom. His agents are on the secret missions to get close and destroy your life and marriage.

The reason our faults and offenses are trigger mechanisms is because we may not like to accept any blame for things, we feel we are not responsible for; therefore, we may proceed to prove our innocence or make our points clear. One thing can lead to another until the house burns down. The fear of the LORD is extremely important in adjusting and welcoming offers of remedial instructions: it will take away the struggle to see yourself as a better person than the other. Even if you know and understand better than the other, your house is not a courtroom and your arguments and disputes are not court matters. Husbands and wives are not lawyers and judges but one family. Forgive one another in love and pray for one another that God may heal and deliver your broken lives.

Confess your faults one to another, and pray one for another, that ye may be healed. The effectual fervent prayer of a righteous man availeth much (James 5:16).

4) Submit one to another:

Submission is not passive and the tenderness of submission as evidence of reverence must not be abused and exploited. A submitted wife is not a victim of abuse and neither is a loving husband! This is why the bridge that holds everything together is the fear of the LORD. The recognition — or acknowledgment of the LORD in the marriage is the key to obeying His laws and adhering to His voice. This is understanding the rule of accountability. Both husband and wife are responsible for one another, and it covers every aspect of their lives. *Submitting yourselves one to another in the fear of God* (Ephesians 5:22). The fear of the LORD is what governs the checks and balances in marriage commitments to make sure everyone is cooperating. Rules are never personal views. Personal views are not enough to carry any marriage through difficult times or challenging situations, especially where there are written laws.

The Bible contains the Testament of the Will of God — it is one of the ways the LORD speaks to you besides hearing His voice and studying the Scriptures is learning important binding principles. The warnings are strategic and the instructions are calculated directives to help you live and win in life including rising above marriage problems. Biblical contents are food for life! The responsibility of marriage is obligatory and you must know what you are getting yourself into, beyond the thrills of marriage ceremonies and the casual recital of the oath or vow of marriage. The statements are affirmative and the commitments are heavy burdens: the road can get tough and very challenging. Your preparedness is the key to surviving the storm. Death is not the only power that can separate or tear a marriage relationship apart; there are other pressures of life that weigh greatly upon the foundation of marriage.

The supporting pillars are the husbands and wives so they must be prepared to fight strategic and tactical battles to save the marriage each day. Looking into the life of your marriage partner will give you a clue of what to expect and beginning the battle before the marriage will save you years of antagonism and aggravation. The makeup of a marriage is not the beautiful looks and even when there are many resources in place, the marriage can still fail. Submitting yourselves one to another in the fear of the LORD will drive both to their knees — seeking for

God's help and intervention in critical situations instead of fighting one another in desperation.

Wives, submit yourselves unto your own husbands, as unto the Lord. For the husband is the head of the wife, even as Christ is the head of the church: and he is the savior of the body. Therefore, as the church is subject unto Christ, so let the wives be to their own husbands in everything. Husbands, love your wives, even as Christ also loved the church, and gave himself for it; That he might sanctify and cleanse it with the washing of water by the word, That he might present it to himself a glorious church, not having spot, or wrinkle, or any such thing; but that it should be holy and without blemish. So, ought men to love their wives as their own bodies. He that loveth his wife loveth himself. For no man ever yet hated his own flesh; but nourisheth and cherisheth it, even as the Lord the church: For we are members of his body, of his flesh, and of his bones. For this cause shall a man leave his father and mother, and shall be joined unto his wife, and they two shall be one flesh (Ephesians 5:22-31).

There is no time in history that the human race has lost touch with spiritual realities than in our generation. Individuals as well as societies have become complacent — ignorant in spiritual things and negligent in adhering to spiritual warnings. We see why the foundations of nations or kingdoms are falling apart. We see why families are crumbling in the heats of deception and lies. We see why people are shaky in their spiritual walks. We see why the Church is part of the world and why carnality has devoured the spiritual backbones of the people of God. The ingredients that fuel spiritual hunger and thirst are no longer considered. The passion for prayer is lost, not only within the Church buildings but also in the family lives. Marriages are suffering today. We have to go back to the grassroots and begin to dig the foundations of our marriages, perhaps we may repair the breaches and start a new life — fully dedicated, committed and sacrificed to the Living God. Faulty foundations are recipes for future disasters. The enemy of our lives will not spear — not even our marriage relationships if we fail to rescue our families and households.

Be ye not unequally yoked together with unbelievers: for what fellowship hath righteousness with unrighteousness? and what communion hath light with darkness? And what concord hath Christ with Belial? or what part hath he that believeth with an infidel? And what agreement hath the temple of God with idols? for ye are the temple of the living God; as God hath said, I will dwell in them, and walk in them; and I will be their God, and they shall be my people. Wherefore come out from among them, and be ye separate, saith the Lord, and touch not the unclean thing; and I will receive you, And will be a Father unto you, and ye shall be my sons and daughters, saith the Lord Almighty (2 Corinthians 6:14-18).

Chapter Ten

REAL FREEDOM

For many people, freedom is a statement, a claim, a confession, a declaration and proclamation! For others, freedom is what they do, the environment and atmosphere, which they function, what they represent or associate with. There are several things that people attach or attribute to freedom, which are short of the real experience of true freedom. Nevertheless, freedom is the state of **being** rather than just singing the song of freedom or claiming to be free. "Whom the Son set free" indicates that there is involvement of work on our parts beyond the sacrifice of Jesus Christ for our sins. The work of freedom is part of the extended processes of the deeper stages of salvation. We must understand that sanctification and consecration are important aspects of realizing our freedom in God. Philippians 2:12 clearly stated that we must *work out our own salvation with fear and trembling before the LORD.* Work here is connotative of making efforts to walk in the statues, principles and obedience to the LORD, including surrendering, submitting and offering our lives wholly unto Him. There are worked-out arrangements that takes us through the paths of possessing or experiencing the reality of our freedom. For many years, we have been taught that freedom is a mere celebration of religious events associated with the works of the cross, but in reality, freedom is reaching for the promises and provisions by doing what is required from us. It is important not to mistake or misplace requirement with personal contribution!

The tendency to replace work for celebration of religious rituals have left many people on the roads to broken dreams. **"Free for real"** is going beyond the belief, the trust and the hope for freedom! I want to show us the pathway to our spiritual and physical inheritances, so that our freedom will no longer remain in the future. **The tagline or subtitle** "Removing the Mask" was birthed from the heart of God. During much prayers, the LORD spoke into my heart concerning His sons and daughters – how to break the cycles of defeat in their lives, and how to experience true freedom that only Him can provide. How many of us really know that the LORD God is Almighty and All-powerful? Whether we know it or not, the LORD desires for you to live a fruitful life, even in the midst of your surroundings and circumstances.

Let us thoroughly examine the opposite of freedom and then, define the word freedom for a better understanding:

By looking at the word **captivity:** it's the state or period of being held, imprisoned, enslaved, or confined. The word **bound:** is to be tied, under legal or moral obligation. Another word is **bondage:** which is the state of being bound by or subjected to some external or internal power or control. **Now, the opposite of bondage is freedom:** Freedom is the state of being free or at liberty rather than confinement or under physical restraint: exemption from external control. The word **real** means: genuine, not counterfeit, authentic, absolute.

When the LORD God made man, he was in the image after His likeness according to Genesis 1:26-27. Man was His carbon copy – a duplicate or a reflection of who He is! We have intellect: a heart to reason thoughtfully, a mind, emotion and will to express ourselves and make our own decisions in life as people! We have the physical body to interact with others. God wanted a people He can personally talk to, reason with, and commune intimately. (See Genesis 3:8). Nevertheless, man bowed to the cunning nature or deception of the devil, who deceived the woman in the form of a serpent. The fall of man was a betrayal of God and as a result of the rebellion, man lost his identity, nature and fellowship with the Father! Ever since the fall, man has become vile, cunning, evil, dangerous, greedy, envious, defiled, polluted, corrupt and sinful!

And GOD saw that the wickedness of man was great in the earth, and that every imagination of the thoughts of his heart was only evil continually (Genesis 6:5).

Jeremiah 17:5 said, *Thus saith the LORD; Cursed be the man that trust in man, and makes flesh his arm, and whose heart departed from the LORD.*

The curse from the fall spread to all mankind and everyone born into this world must deal with the power of curses:

Romans 5:12 said, *Wherefore, as by one man sin entered into the world, and death by sin; and so death passed upon all men, for that all have sinned.*

It's no surprise that evil, sin and immorality abound around us and we can easily get caught up in the web of man's savagery and wickedness. We are all stuck with having to deal with issues arising from the fall of the first man. All of us have and will continue to deal with the reality of evil pervading every sphere of our existence. Our lives have one way or another been impacted and deeply affected by the product of that great fall. There will always remain those who by their own will have chosen to continue to express their evil tendencies. It should not be a surprise to us when we get hurt to some extent or degree. We are in a world that is ruled by pure evil! No person can conclusively say that he or she has not experienced some form of evil, wickedness and hurt in this life. One thing sure is that the dosage may not be the same: some people have gone through different levels of pain, hurt and traumatic events. Some people's experiences are mild compared to the others; however, regardless of what happened, mankind will continue to go through such experiences in life. It is in the nature of those who are under demonic powers to continue to do evil. (See 1 John 3:8a). We are witnessing evil being committed against fellow men today in every society. When we listen around us, every second someone is being robbed, raped, murdered, abducted, abused, terrorized, deceived, lied against, manipulated and much more. It is almost impossible to go a day without hearing bad news being reported on our news media. There are other countless incidents that are never even mentioned or reported. We must understand that we are in a war-zone, and we are faced with daily chaos!

1 Corinthians 15:22 said, *For as in Adam all die, even so in Christ shall all be made alive.*

I want to help someone, even if it were one person! God desires for His children to free from the dictation of the flesh and the power of sin. We must come to the place where we remove all disguises and cover-ups. Some of us hide behind titles, money, clothes, jobs, careers, degrees and other achievements or accomplishments, etc. They never experienced wholeness because of secret proclivities that have hindered their spiritual growth and maturity. God is looking to do something new in people's lives everywhere if they are willing to allow Him to step into the hidden parts, they have not given access to anyone. God is gentle and He waits for a formal invitation rather than aggressively intrude. He can heal, deliver, restore, change and transform our whole lives.

In order to be free, you must first find your true identity, which is the key to personal authenticity. Your unique ability is divinely placed and made part of your life as the Creator's original plan. This is why you do not have to compete with anyone because God never want you to become a copy of someone else. He has designed you with a different makeup unlike any other person on the face of the Earth. He takes pleasure in the true essence of who He has made you to be. I want you to embrace a new mindset as you read through this important material. You have to understand that your lifestyle can never rise above the level of your mentality. Therefore, your mind must be renewed and your life must be changed by the Holy Spirit for you to reach where God is taking you. Always remember that whole transformation is going beyond levels of change processes!

You must get real to be made whole:

1. Real with yourself

2. Real with people
3. Real with the LORD God

Many people are walking time-bombs in our societies today because real issues in their lives are not being addressed. Some of these issues are relative to their personal lives, family relationships, spouses or other people in general. Sweeping things under the rug will only complicate matters and cause the problems to remain unchecked. Always, Jesus will reach down to the roots of our conditions – it is to show that He ultimately desires to build a brand-new foundation in our lives. Therefore, it is our responsibility to carefully break free from unhealthy habits and attitude dispositions that can affect our breakthroughs.

There are conditions that are attached to the promises of God, which we must exercise caution to observe and to do them:

Deuteronomy 28:1 said, *And it shall come to pass, if thou shalt hearken diligently unto the voice of the LORD thy God, to observe and to do all his commandments which I command thee this day, that the LORD thy God will set thee on high above all nations of the earth.*

The word **"overtake"** in the Greek context means to tackle, chase after you, and to grasp you so that you fall. It simply shows the blessing will chase you down. The LORD wants to release His spiritual and physical rain of blessings upon your life. He wants you to bear much fruit! Please take some time to read verses 2 through verse 9 of Deuteronomy Chapter 28. From verse 1 through verse 14 are about the blessings that will come upon you, if you carefully obey the voice of the LORD God. Verse 15 through 68 are about the curses if you disobey the voice of the LORD God.

I want you to ask yourself these important questions, what are the things that are keeping you away from reaching your high place in God:

- Is it Lust?
- Is it Bitterness?
- Is it Anger?
- Is it Pride?
- Is it Materialism?
- Is it Greed?
- Is it Divorce?
- Is it Jealousy?
- Is it Envy?
- Is it Unforgiveness?
- Is it Idolatry?
- Is it Devils?
- Is it Family and Friends?
- Is it Life?

What bondage is stopping your fruitfulness? What proclivity is hindering you from moving in God's great authority and power? What sin, iniquity, trespass and transgression are perpetuating your situation and stopping you from seeing God's breakthrough in your life? Adultery is the sin, but lust is the iniquity – the inward bent! Lust is part of what is hidden in the heart!

Jesus said, *For out of the heart proceed evil thoughts, murders, adulteries, fornications, thefts, false witness, blasphemies* (See Matthew 12:35; 15:19).

Psalms 44:21 said, *Shall not God search this out? for he knoweth the secrets of the heart.*

Numbers 14:18 records: *The LORD is longsuffering, and of great mercy, forgiving iniquity and transgression, and by no means clearing the guilty, visiting the iniquity of the fathers upon the children unto the third and fourth generation.*

Jeremiah 29:32 said, *Therefore thus saith the LORD; Behold, I will punish Shemaiah the Nehelamite, and his seed: he shall not have a man to dwell among this people; neither shall he behold the good that I will do for my people, saith the LORD; because he hath taught rebellion against the LORD.*

I want you to look at this carefully:

If they shall confess their iniquity, and the iniquity of their fathers, with their trespass which they trespassed against me, and that also they have walked contrary unto me (Leviticus 26:40).

God said: *I call heaven and earth to record this day against you, that I have set before you life and death, blessing and cursing: therefore choose life, that both thou and thy seed may live: That thou mayest love the LORD thy God, and that thou mayest obey his voice, and that thou mayest cleave unto him: for he is thy life, and the length of thy days: that thou mayest dwell in the land which the LORD swore unto thy fathers, to Abraham, to Isaac, and to Jacob, to give them* (Deuteronomy 30:19-20).

There is hope for the people of God today! It is why you are reading this material to experience real healing and deliverance – real change and whole transformation.

Here is a clear warning for us:

1. We must refuse to twist and misinterpret the Word of God to fit what we want.
2. We must come to a place where we deliberately quit from acting like everything is perfect when we know fully that we are in the brink of suicide.
3. We must decisively confront our problems and dare to challenge our fears.
4. We must be willing to take calculated risks according to the Word of God and sincerely ask the Holy Spirit to help us.
5. We cannot be victorious and triumphant by accepting the status quo.

The reason we want generational curses, habits and addictions, patterns, and other negative impacts to be destroyed in our lives is because they are handicapping and paralyzing the progress of our purpose and destiny. Some of us will have to forgive where we have been wronged before we can move forward. You may not know what to do on your own! The good news is that the Holy Spirit is here to help you do what you could not do otherwise! Until you are tired of performing and acting, God will not move to empower you to break free. You cannot conquer and overcome what you never dared to confront or challenge.

Some people are hiding behind the masks: labels, titles and positions. Some people are in wrong relationships because they are wounded and desperate: they have not been affirmed and confirmed – validated and approved, so they keep searching for men and women, drugs, sex, alcohols and other substance abuse to fill the void that only God alone can heal and deliver them from the damages. We have to know that we cannot fool God nor satan but

ourselves and others. God wants to set us free from belief systems and perspectives that are not in line with the
truth of His Word. Spiritual conviction is part of bringing us into alliance and complaint with the Word of God.
There are character traits that are dangerously crippling
our purpose and destiny, and some of them are those
things we have been taught. We may not be responsible
for what happened to us in life; however, we must take responsibility because we are accountable for how we process and deal with what happened.

**Some of us must learn how to properly resolve
conflicts:**

- No more false pretenses
- No more blaming others
- No more hurting others through sick cycles

Jesus Christ came to heal the brokenhearted:

*The Spirit of the Lord is upon me, because he hath anoint-
ed me to preach the gospel to the poor; he hath sent me to
heal the brokenhearted, to preach deliverance to the captives,
and recovering of sight to the blind, to set at liberty them that
are bruised, To preach the acceptable year of the Lord* (Luke
4:18-19).

We must cease to project images of false protection
when we know for a fact that we really need help in our
lives. Some people are waiting for special apologies from
those who did them wrong. The question is, can you move
forward even if you never get an apology? You cannot
build until you begin to pluck up and destroy the old foundation and structures. Everywhere today, there are frustration, anger, hate, bitterness, proclivities and bondage.

In our relationships, there must be:

1. No more stage-playing
2. No more theatrical adventures
3. No more acting
4. No more hiding behind personal achievements and accomplishments or the lack thereof, etc.

God wants to your spirit, soul and body completely whole – fulfilled and walking in your divine purpose and destiny. God will give you power to remain stable in a chaotic society. God is looking to rebuild and restore your life with His great love. We need people that will not lie to us – those who will stretch and push us beyond where we are. We need brilliant minds that will provoke our brilliance – stir us up to get to our next dimensions in God. God desires for us to move from glory-to-glory or deeper revelation after deeper revelation in the realms of the spirit. Church is truly a hospital for people! If something is wrong, you visit medical doctors to get the problem addressed or corrected. You must know that like in the natural so also in the spiritual. 1 Peter 5:8 said, *Be sober, be vigilant; because your adversary the devil, as a roaring lion, walketh about, seeking whom he may devour.* The above Scripture is very clear: the enemy cannot devour everyone except those who are not spiritually prepared – trained and equipped. We have so much negative influences in our world today. The enemy wants to use every possible artifice to distract, confuse, deter and trip us to fall. He wants us to open the doors of our lives for him to enter and possess our temple – the temple of God! Even if we are comfortable in our bondage, we need someone to shake us out of it. If Christians cannot be in bondage, the question then is, why did Jesus call deliverance the children's bread? We have to understand that the Kingdom of heaven takes violent force. (See Matthew 11:12). Great authority and power are necessary to achieve and maintain freedom.

Some of us need to undergo deliverance in one area or more areas of our lives. Deliverance is another form of spiritual warfare that deals with addressing areas of bondage in a person's life. It may be bloodline curses involving ancestral and generational issues. It could be marital, witchcraft, occultic and other links or attachments that are connected to us, and must take the authority and power of Jesus Christ to break free. Deliverance deals with a person's foundation that control the physical life. The things we cannot stop doing means that we are passing them to the generational line to affect our children. Therefore, it is imperative that you prepare for your deliverance! You do not have to remain oppressed, bound, scarred, wounded, hurt, yoked up and living in fear all your life! *If the Son therefore shall make you free, ye shall be free indeed* (John 8:36).

Jesus came so that we can experience real authentic freedom, but very often, we never address the hidden matters of the heart. We live for years and never take off the mask. Nevertheless, only when we take off the mask that we can truly discover who we really are, in Him. We must endeavor to confront the painful issues whether past or present that plague us day-in and day-out! We need to put off the mask and begin to cry out to the LORD God for our freedom through Jesus Christ. I am here as your mid-wife, to help you to push harder in the spirit and bring forth your vision that the enemy had stolen. You are a promised-child, marked for the great blessing of the LORD God!

Shall the prey be taken from the mighty, or the lawful captive delivered? But thus saith the LORD, Even the captives of the mighty shall be taken away, and the prey of the terrible shall be delivered: for I will contend with him that contendeth with thee, and I will save thy children. And I will feed them that oppress thee with their own flesh; and they shall be drunken with their own blood, as with sweet wine: and all flesh shall know that I the LORD am thy Saviour and thy Redeemer, the mighty One of Jacob (Isaiah 49:24-26).

Chapter Eleven

ROLE OF THE HOLY SPIRIT

The Book of John 4:24 revealed a powerful secret about the person of God: The Bible said, God is a Spirit — a being without flesh and blood or human. With the manifestation of Jesus Christ as a man (1 John 3:8), the Bible said that God took the form of a man (Philippians 2:7), but God as a spirit-being is not a man (Numbers 23:19). It is extremely important to gather as much intelligence on who the Holy Spirit really is, if we are going to understand His role in life, not just only the believers' lives.

Nevertheless, I tell you the truth; It is expedient for you that I go away: for if I go not away, the Comforter will not come unto you; but if I depart, I will send him unto you. And when he is come, he will reprove the world of sin, and of righteousness, and of judgment (John 16:7-8).

Then Peter said unto them, Repent, and be baptized every one of you in the name of Jesus Christ for the remission of sins, and ye shall receive the gift of the Holy Ghost. For the promise is unto you, and to your children, and to all that are afar off, even as many as the Lord our God shall call (Acts 2:38-39).

Before we proceed to unearth the intricate works of the Holy Spirit, we have to show certain symbolic typification, manifestations and other representations to draw from their respective meanings as they relate to the life of the Holy Spirit. Symbols that typify or represent His characteristic behaviors and manifestations are keys to unlocking some of His real-life personifications as well as His attributes. Together, they form the backbone of clearer understanding of Him as a person. The makeup of a person is not only the behavioral patterns, but also how he or she reacts to changes and what those changes mean to his or her life. A person cannot be mistaken for one of his or her behaviors or how he or she responded to a particular situation. A person cannot be misplaced for a thing or inanimate object. This is why character and manifestations offer us alternative charts to derive our investigation even if we do not share a particular level of closeness with the person of the Holy Spirit. We are carefully examining who He is, versus what He does, so we will better articulate His manifestations — His presence and power in our lives.

- In Genesis 1:2, He is the Spirit of God
- Psalms 51:11; Ephesians 1:13; 4:30, He is the Holy Spirit
- Psalms 51:12, He is the Free Spirit
- Isaiah 4:4, 11:3, He is the Spirit of Judgment
- Isaiah 11:1, He is the Spirit of the LORD
- Isaiah 11:2, He is the Spirit of Knowledge
- He is the Spirit of Understanding
- He is the Spirit of Wisdom
- He is the Spirit of Counsel
- He is the Spirit of Might
- He is the Spirit of the fear of the LORD

- Isaiah 61:1, He is the Spirit of the LORD God
- Zechariah 12:10, He is the Spirit of Grace
- Matthew 10:20, He is the Spirit of the Father
- Luke 1:35, He is the Power of the Highest — Omnipotent
- John 14:16, He is the Comforter
- Romans 1:4, He is the Spirit of Holiness
- Romans 8:2, He is the Spirit of Life
- Romans 8:15, He is the Spirit of Adoption
- Galatians 4:6, He is the Spirit of the Son
- Hebrews 9:14, He is the Eternal Spirit
- 2 Timothy 1:7, He is the Spirit of Love
- He is the Spirit of Power
- He is the Spirit of a Sound Mind
- 1 Peter 1:11, He is the Spirit of Christ
- 1 Peter 4:14, He is the Spirit of Glory
- Revelation 19:10, He is the Spirit of Prophecy

We are seeing a chart of His personalities mixed with His special abilities or what He can do with His power. It is important to underline these behaviors and manifestations to be able to fully connect with Him unless we do not understand His roles in our lives as Christians. The behaviors that define His characteristic are keys to the changes necessary in your Christian life and likewise, His abilities bring the enabling capacity to help you fulfill the mandatory work of the LORD. Because the Church does not understand the Holy Spirit, there are shortages of real prepared Christians around the world; instead, we are seeing deformed systems that are plagued by disabilities. We are seeing professing Christians that are unable to live the life of Christ and do the works of Jesus Christ. Although Church buildings are erected everywhere, the workings of Christ are nowhere to be experienced. This is where going back to the drawing-board is so urgent because time is of the essence. The Holy Spirit has distinctive roles besides the works of the cross through Jesus Christ. What many of us often forget is that without the Holy Spirit, Christ would not have been able to accomplish those demanding tasks of the Father. Coming in the volumes of the Book will require the life and power of the Spirit or what is written cannot be fulfilled. This is what happened with the law — the practice of rehearsing the law led to breaking the law rather than doing the law.

We must not be careless to mistake the person of the Holy Spirit or misplace His roles in our Christian lives. There is no true Christianity without the Spirit of God, even if we know all the Scriptures from Genesis to Revelation including every other material. The word "Christian" covers beyond our confessions and statements of faith — it is living the life of Jesus Christ and the absence of the Holy Spirit is absence of Christianity. Salvation is practical engagements and applications of the provisions of the works of the cross; therefore, merely participating in religious activities cannot substantiate nor fulfill Christian experiences. As the Spirit of God, we cannot interact with God in a personal relationship without the Holy Spirit. The Holy Spirit is a descriptive term to emphasize on the nature of His purity — He is non-defiling like demonic spirits. This is the way to judge between His character and evil spirits.

The Holy Spirit cannot lead you into unrighteous, unholy, unclean and defiled lifestyle because His life is not contradictory to what is written in the Testament of the Will of God. It is the reason His life and power are the keys to fulfilling the Will and purpose of God for your life. In other words, He brings the change and ability you need to live and achieve whatever the LORD God has ordained for you to do. The Spirit of God is not the spirit of bondage — as the free Spirit, He brings the application of the provisions of the works of the cross to liberate you from all enemy captivity and bondage. Always, freedom takes more than a declaration or pronouncement: there are things that are required and until they are fulfilled, our freedom will remain on hold. Where the Spirit of the LORD is, there is liberty or the expression of true freedom, not just the confession of freedom. The hope of freedom and being free are altogether different. The Spirit of the LORD God is the one that delivers and sets the people of God free. Preaching, teaching and every other religious activity are ineffective without the power of the Holy Spirit. (See Isaiah 61:1-3; Luke 4:18-19). Although practice makes perfect, we must remember that practice leads to many failures.

The seven manifestations of the Spirit show how the power of God becomes active in our lives. Some people of God mistake the processes of God for religious order of events and they risk unfruitful Christian life by damping down the important works of the Holy Spirit. Power is transmittable depending on the source of power. Life application is not the same with mechanical application. The contingencies of the manifested presence of the Holy Spirit and the power of God are to show how both the life and power of God are interconnected, so we must understand that we cannot manufacture the presence and power of God. As the Spirit of knowledge, understanding, wisdom, counsel, might, fear of the LORD and judgment, it is evident that these important spiritual abilities cannot be mimicked or easily achieved through many other sources. The life and power of God always remained the life and power of God, so it is not something that people can run to many other places and get the life and power of God. The Spirit of the LORD or the LORD God is an indicator to establish the source. Acts 1:8 said, ye shall receive power after that the Holy Spirit has come upon you. Acts 10:38 confirmed how the power of God is released by the Spirit of God. The role of the Holy Spirit is to bring change and enhancements into the believers' life until whole transformation. The farther we follow His leadership is the deeper we will experience the Living God. The whole character and attributes of God are realized in our lives through the life and power of the Holy Spirit. Many things we attribute to great success are often lacking the spiritual qualities that magnify us and our works before the LORD. The reason is that everything is examined in the light of life and power of the Spirit beyond personal estimation or appreciation.

The Holy Spirit is given to the believers, who are adopted through Jesus Christ. Adoption is going from one family line into another to be raised up according to a new cultural standard of life. We have to see that the works of the Holy Spirit does not stop on Earth: He continues to work to bring our lives to fit into the life of the LORD God and the Kingdom of Heaven. Until we recognize the urgency of the works of the Holy Spirit in our lives, we will unconsciously undermine the completed works of the cross. We will have a Christianity without being Christians. We will live and function in defeat and failures rather than seeing the fulfillment of God's great promises in our lives. Provisions without application leads to zero or negative balance, which is the reason people confess and claim their breakthroughs for many years without receiving their breakthroughs. Working out your salvation is working out things according to the finished works of the cross to bring the applications into your life. And you must not forget that the Holy Spirit is the application of the Will of God — without the Holy Spirit, you cannot fulfill the criteria to live according to the Will nor do the Will. As He conditions ourselves according to the Will, He will help prepare us to receive the blessings. The Bible said, if you pray according to His Will, but please understand that praying is one thing, you must also do the Will. The way spiritual credits are earned is by the approval of the Holy Spirit. Many things we see today are coercion — they are manipulated and controlled to represent a spiritual milestone without enduring through the processes to be fitted according to divine orders. We may think that God is winking but readiness takes preparedness!

Because the Holy Spirit was purposefully sent on a mission in the body of Christ, we must look beyond personal expertise and other expectations. We must see that anything that takes learning and training requires surrender and submission. We must see temporary accord as a thin-line between make or break. The union of two people is like walking on a tight-rope. Agreement is not always as easy as paperwork. We can agree to disagree and frustrating the works of the Holy Spirit is retiring before you even report for the job. It is missing all that is there to succeed. The Holy Spirit is the leader of the true Church of Jesus Christ, and every called leader or local Church that rejects the Holy Spirit will lack the legitimate equipping to move the people forward. We are in the age of stagnation and regression — where people are moving in circles or going backwards because there is no forwardness. The Church has wasted many years, but we must move quickly to correct things or fail to catch up with the end-times spiritual momentum. The Holy Spirit is ever willing to lead and He will continue to lead until the very end!

Part of the special work of the Holy Spirit is to impact the conscience, the thought and imagination to bring the awareness and conviction of sexual sin. Therefore, we must know that the Holy Spirit does not recommend pornography and masturbation or lead us to other sexual materials and contents. Lust and perversion are different from normal sexual feeling within a marriage bed. Because the bed must not be defiled, the Holy Spirit cannot lead married believers into the beds of adultery or single believers into the beds of fornication. There are numerous other pervasive sexual behaviors that people engage in the acts or expose their lives. The Holy Spirit is trusted with fulfilling the Will of God as the co-Author of the Bible. Leading us according to the Testament of the Will of God is why the inspiration of the Holy Spirit references the Word for divine accuracy.

The Will is written to reveal the law of God concerning certain behaviors that breach the guidelines for Christian lifestyle. Parts of spiritual convictions are exposing all contradictions whether in material forms or personal characteristics. He will warn you whenever you trespass into such thresholds. The Holy Spirit will not lead us into inordinate affections and attractions that are contrary to the recommendations of the written Will of God. Always, the written Will, the inspiration of the Spirit and the revelation of God agree. Fornication and adultery regardless of what types of relationships and sexual preferences are sinful before God. All acts of unrighteousness are sin and all forms of immoral behaviors are sin. Sexual sin is against the body and our body is the temple of the Holy Spirit; therefore, the Holy Spirit will not lead us into sexual sin. Sin generally is contrary to the nature of God — or who the Holy Spirit is, as the Spirit of the LORD God.

Then Peter said unto them, Repent, and be baptized every one of you in the name of Jesus Christ for the remission of sins, and ye shall receive the gift of the Holy Ghost. For the promise is unto you, and to your children, and to all that are afar off, even as many as the Lord our God shall call (Acts 2:38-39).

Chapter Twelve

REASON TO WAIT

Do you know that it is ideal for every unmarried — single person to wait before engaging in sexual activities? If you are about to commence a relationship but you are unsure about how to deal with the sexual aspect, I want you to know that you can be in a relationship without opening yourself to sexuality. Sex is ordained by God to take place between a man (husband) and woman (wife). Sexual intercourse is a beautiful aspect of marriage! God has blessed us with the ability to give and receive physical pleasure from sexual intimacy as husband and wife. Nevertheless, sex is turned into another thing when we offer ourselves to another person outside of marriage.

In the earlier days of my life, it was a taboo to openly discuss sexual matters with either friends or even the opposite sex. Today, everything has changed! Sex is much more confusing in our generation than ever before. Sex adds great pressure to new relationships and it does not get easier as we grow older. Nevertheless, for the security and protection of our relationship, we must freely discuss the issues of sex with our marriage partners. The

SPIRITUAL SIDE OF SEX

modern society has encouraged sex among the unmarried — young and old, instead of teaching them to wait until after marriage. Incidents like one-night-stands has become a way to have fun without regards to dangerous consequences. There are numerous reasons why unmarried singles should wait until marriage before engaging in sexual activities.

One may ask, how can something that feels so good be so wrong to do? Some people may also question, isn't being in a committed relationship the same as being married? All across the world, many people are faced with these pressing questions when it comes to making the decision whether or not to have sex. It is hard to say no to sexual contact when people are supposedly in love, engaged, have an attraction and affection for someone or committed to him or her in a relationship. The question is, why should I wait?

Here some keys you must consider:

Lust and Fornication are Sins: when unmarried people or singles engage in sexual contact, it is called fornication. We must understand that our feelings must be carefully guarded from lust and perversion. There is a stop-sign that lust and perversion can take our feelings beyond to hemorrhage our spiritual purpose and destiny. Sex is more than having a feeling. It is more than having fun. Sexual contact before marriage may be enjoyable for the moment but the pain will hurt later. Multiple sex partners will bring great pain in your life because of multiple soulties, sex-ties and demonic captivity and bondage. The Will of God for every unmarried — single person is to be mentally, emotionally and spiritually pure before and after marriage. Part of the great expectation of marriage is the unveiling of the bride and groom — the opening of the purity of his or her life to one another. It is like turning the first page or a journey into a promised land.

Virginity is a Special Gift for a Husband or Wife: any husband would appreciate the chastity and purity of his wife. The same applies to the wife. A chaste virgin is like an alabaster jar or oil of the apothecaries. Virginity is a language of innocence: it is a testimony of spiritual and physical fidelity. Purity has aromatizing scent like a fragrance, even as pollution and defilement exudes foul odors. Sharing your sexual life for the first time with your husband or wife is achieving a monumental history. It is infusing into a sacred oath — sealed with beauty and purity. Chasity is a spiritual value that comes with spiritual reward. If you have lost your virginity, you must repent sincerely before the LORD and break all the ties and blood covenant or initiation. You must be free and whole to enjoy your future husband or wife. Broken marriages are evidences of defilement and sabotages whether from the enemy or our own misdeeds besides family and friends. Some people of God don't understand why dating is a snare: you cannot put fire in your bosom without getting burned. It is important to share friendship with other people of God who understand the dangers of sexual sin. Flee from sexual sin! Making room for the flesh will help you to fall! You must protect your heart against all unwanted intrusions.

Virginity is like having a precious ornament or gem: finding a man or woman that will remain a virgin until after marriage in our modern day, even among professing Christians is a miraculous work of God. The temple of God is filled with temple prostitutes – concubines devoted to the idols of false kings and rulers – priests and priestesses in the house of God. There is no time that the house of the LORD has been desecrated – defiled and polluted by the modern-day king Davids and Solomons of our generation. We have temple gods and goddesses sacrificed to temple priests, priestesses, kings and rulers, who sabotage the orders of God's sacred worship. Righteousness and holiness today are not great preaching because the messages of "grace" "prosperity" and "come as you are" have corrupted the mindset of the innocent seekers of the true Living God. The Church has become a system and a trading block where everything is up for sale, including the virginity of the sons and daughters of God. Virgins are no longer sitting under the coverings of prayers in the Churches, instead they are raped and molested – reduced to PRs to fight against the exposures of the proclivities of temple idols called ministers and leaders. We understand that it is not easy to remain focused and committed to a lifestyle of chastity in the midst of extraordinary distraction and deception.

It is not easy to stay a virgin when sex is a modern-day high commodity. I must commend and recommend anyone who dares to raise up the banner and pass the touch to the next generation. There is absolutely nothing amazing about defiling yourself in the fornication bed before marriage or jumping in the bed of adultery after marriage. Any older woman that is experienced in life will admonish you to wait until after marriage! Always, feeling, attraction, affection and love are separate. As people of God, our focus should be on what the LORD God wants for our lives rather than the society: family, friends and associates, etc. Anything that is contrary to the words of Jesus Christ should never be a part of our Christian life! God's original plan for His people is to remain pure for marriage. There are consequential retributions when we violate the commandment of the LORD for our lives. Some people's disobedience has led to sicknesses, diseases, unwanted pregnancies and other soul-ties. The choices we make in life carry heavy penalties until we realize that life and foolishness are not compatible! We must seek after the Will of God concerning everything in our lives.

It is common for strangers to share sexual intimacy today in this careless and carefree generation without knowing the history or background of their sexual partners. Sexual contact is not intimacy per say, the mode in which the intercourse occur is what makes it intimate or it's only a reaction to the flame of lust and perversion. Casual sex is risking your life at the edge of death! Unmarried people – singles should learn to wait until they are married before engaging in sexual activities. As Christians, our friendships are cultivated upon the foundation of honor, respect and love of God. Marriage is made of mental, emotional, spiritual and sexual respect!

Unwanted Pregnancy: Always, we hear that children are the gift of the LORD. They are special blessings to families, but there are things we must consider as people of God when it comes to raising up children. We must understand that children are a responsibility and from spiritual standpoint, bound woman also produce bound offspring. What it means is that there are children conceived out of marriage covenants. Promise children like Isaac have spiritual promise and inheritance. Raising children in the admonition of the LORD is the key to establishing them upon spiritual principles. When they grow up, they will not depart or abandon the way of the LORD. Besides, spiritual responsibilities there are physical responsibility in caring for the children. God wants us to be prepared both spiritually and physically to raise up our children and this is how He rewards our efforts by releasing His blessings upon our families. Having children out of wed-lock or committing an abortion are both unreasonable and unfair for both the parents and the children. This is why abstinence is sacrificial but very rewarding, and hav-ing children after marriage is part of securing the futures of the children from spiritual and physical challenges of life. God wants us to be mentally, emotionally and spiritu-ally prepared to undertake the responsibility of raising up our children.

Dating/Match-Making Can Lead to Disaster: Sexual intimacy frames the mental, emotional and spiritual state of a person. There is an interconnection – an attachment that zig-zag across the terrains of the inner parts of the human beings. The connection is not easily broken by therapy or counseling because it reaches the depth of life in the spirit realms. What we have to look at is that many dating/match-making relationships are not joined in the love of God. Often, affection and attraction are like smokescreens; therefore, everybody is there for their own interest or what they can gain temporarily. There is no passion for long-term commitment and investment. This is why it can easily lead to disaster and heart-troubles. When the affection and attraction begin to fade or what-ever helped glued the relationship together starts to tear apart, the parties will make a quick dash to escape the tsu-nami that is about to hit the foundation. People can decide to leave the relationship simply because they are bored or distracted by something more promising. The right mind-set, the right emotion and the right mental state as well as spiritual depth are important in comprehending and ful-filling God's purpose and destiny for our lives. Dating/match-making is going in the opposite direction of the spiritual guidance of the LORD. It is taking a detour from the Holy Spirit!

The Purpose of Sex: God's purpose for sex was to re-
produce — create an extended family, although sexual
intercourse in itself is pleasurable. In Genesis 1:22, the
LORD God commanded the first family to increase and
multiply. Man and woman are uniquely designed to enjoy
sexual intimacy with one another and spiritual and physical bonding takes place when a husband and wife share
sexual contact. The effect of what they feel a day after sex
may differ.

What Happens When You Have Sex: one of the hor-
mones released during sexual intercourse is oxytocin,
which causes a person to desire to touch and be touched.
Oxytocin also causes a person to become emotionally and
physically bonded together. Therefore, both the man and
woman feel close to the respective partner after sexual intercourse. The man on the other hand produces vasopres-
sin, which causes him to feel responsible for the woman
he shared sexual intimacy with. This is good or fruitful in
a marital relationship. The last thing a single man wants
to do is feel responsible for a woman he is casually dating.
In some cases, the feeling of responsibility may even help
drive the man away if he is not seriously willing to commit
to marriage relationship. Because of the hormonal interactions, a woman usually feels clingier after sexual contact while a man may seem somewhat distant.

Pregnancy and Sexually Transmitted Disease: people
often have wrong conception of protection and security
when it comes sexually transmitted disease. They feel
that because they used condoms, they are safe in some
manner from contracting STDs. The truth however is that
condoms are not one hundred percent effective. They can
break during sexual intercourse. They can leak. They can

also slide off. And sometimes, people may forget to put on condoms during sexual contacts. Some people may use condoms during the initial start of their relationship but later on, as they become familiar, they may cease to continue to advocate such precautions. The unsafe measures can immediately lead to unexpected or unwanted pregnancy or even acquiring STDs. We must be serious about sexually transmitted diseases! Looking at the statistics will show that the human race is already in great danger everywhere because of the impacts of STDs. If we think about herpes, gonorrhea, syphilis, chlamydia and AIDS, etc., some of the people who contracted these diseases may not know that they are positive. It is estimated that one in every four people have herpes.

Either sexual partner can transmit these diseases to the other partner. Herpes compromises your immune system and make you more vulnerable to contract other STDS or even AIDS. Black women are disproportionately affected by AIDS virus. Now, we must exercise caution because it seems as there are patterns of categorizing people of color to be more prone to different viruses or sicknesses and diseases. And this may be part of an agenda! Sicknesses and diseases are not discriminatory and neither do they have any preference. African-Americans are said to be only thirteen percent of the population but they are responsible for about fifty-one present of new AIDS diagnoses. Black men are said to be diagnosed at the rate of more than seven times the white and black women. Black women are diagnosed at the rate of twenty times than white women. We must see the risk every time we expose ourselves to sexual activities regardless of whether it is oral or anal sexual behaviors.

The exchange of bodily fluids is open risk of contracting STDS. You must never depend on condoms to do all the works for you: you must deliberately protect yourself. There are some people that desire to have children, perhaps one day. The question you must answer is, do you really want to have a child with the person you are dating — or casually having sex with? Do you really desire to be a single parent? Do you believe there will be some type of support even for the child? There are single parents both fathers and mothers struggling everywhere to raise their children and the psychological impacts on the children and families are enormous. Even if all the resources — materially are there, we must think hard before having children. The only sure-fire protection against STDS, AIDS and pregnancy besides other spiritual implications and legal complications is hundred percent abstinence.

Other Important Factors Before Sex

Wrong Image: one of the several reasons why you must endeavor to avoid sexual contact is to save your image. You must never project a wrong image of yourself to reduce your standard. A man or woman may limit their commitments to the relationship or categorize you as only a woman or a man fit for a girlfriend and boyfriend. You may be seen as someone who is not a marriage type! If you are only seeking after a boyfriend and girlfriend status, you must carefully wait before jumping into sexual activities. Very critical to set boundaries to safeguard your life!

Eliminating Procedure: regardless of how you may look at it, there are some men and women who desire only sexual contact. It is important that you safeguard your sexual purity — avoid any rush to sexual exploration and exploitation. This is how to end the relationship on a clear note in the case of sudden breakdown. Close the room against personal victimization!

Cultivate a Deeper Relationship: jumping into illicit sexual contact is not the secret to building a deeper wholesome relationship. There are spiritual and physical prerequisites that must add to the foundational trust-building beyond any personal assessments, feelings and desires. A relationship is more than attraction and affection, so you must proceed with disciplinary caution or the relationship will fail the test!

Sex is God's Plan: God created sex so that two people can share intimate experience in marriage relationship. Sex is a perfect bonding experience to help marriage grow strong: the couples' bond with one another and create a loving home environment for the children. Becoming one flesh is exposing a spiritual connection beyond physical fantasy. 1 Corinthians Chapter 6 reminds us that we are joined as one flesh with whomsoever we share sexual contact. The Scripture went further to explain that all other sins are committed outside the body, but sexual intercourse outside of marriage is sin against our own body. I am persuaded that you would not want to purposefully or intentionally harm yourself! Remember that sex causes a person to become physically, emotionally and spiritually joined with the other person. It does not matter if you wished you never met your sexual partner. It does not matter how you were treated in the relationship, and it does not matter if you remained friends or went your separate ways, the fact is, you are connected.

This is why you must deal with the soul-ties, the sex-ties and the demonic ties — you must break all the covenants, initiations, links, attachments, associations and altars. I want you to think about it carefully in case of another time you may be faced with the decision to engage in sexual activities. You must choose to honor and respect yourself and the person involved by honoring the LORD above the pleasures of strange sexual encounters. Protect yourself mentally, emotionally and spiritually! You are responsible for your own life; therefore, do everything to protect yourself. There is beauty in waiting. You increase your worth in the eyes of your partner as a man or woman of honor, dignity and respect. Wait and surprise your partner on your wedding night with the gift of your virginity and purity! Speak the language of innocence through your virginity and purity in your marriage bed, instead of defiling and polluting your life! Many relationships are not ready for the future because the past has not yet vacated the scene!

Important Scriptures for Consideration:

That ye abstain from meats offered to idols, and from blood, and from things strangled, and from fornication: from which if ye keep yourselves, ye shall do well. Fare ye well (Acts 15:29).

As touching the Gentiles which believe, we have written and concluded that they observe no such thing, save only that they keep themselves from things offered to idols, and from blood, and from strangled, and from fornication (Acts 21:25).

Being filled with all unrighteousness, fornication, wickedness, covetousness, maliciousness; full of envy, murder, debate, deceit, malignity; whisperers (Romans 1:29).

It is reported commonly that there is fornication among you, and such fornication as is not so much as named among the Gentiles, that one should have his father's wife (1 Corinthians 5:1).

Meats for the belly, and the belly for meats: but God shall destroy both it and them. Now the body is not for fornication, but for the Lord; and the Lord for the body (1 Corinthians 6:13).

Nevertheless, to avoid fornication, let every man have his own wife, and let every woman have her own husband (1 Corinthians 7:2).

Neither let us commit fornication, as some of them committed, and fell in one day three and twenty thousand (1 Corinthians 10:8).

And lest, when I come again, my God will humble me among you, and that I shall bewail many which have sinned already, and have not repented of the uncleanness and fornication and lasciviousness which they have committed (2 Corinthians 12:21).

But fornication, and all uncleanness, or covetousness, let it not be once named among you, as becometh saints (Ephesians 5:3).

Now the works of the flesh are manifest, which are these; Adultery, fornication, uncleanness, lasciviousness (Galatians 5:19).

Mortify therefore your members which are upon the earth; fornication, uncleanness, inordinate affection, evil concupiscence, and covetousness, which is idolatry (Colossians 3:5).

For this is the will of God, even your sanctification, that ye should abstain from fornication (1 Thessalonians 4:3).

Even as Sodom and Gomorrah, and the cities about them in like manner, giving themselves over to fornication, and going after strange flesh, are set forth for an example, suffering the vengeance of eternal fire (Jude 1:7).

But I have a few things against thee, because thou hast there them that hold the doctrine of Balaam, who taught Balak to cast a stumbling block before the children of Israel, to eat things sacrificed unto idols, and to commit fornication (Revelation 2:14).

Notwithstanding I have a few things against thee, because thou sufferest that woman Jezebel, which calleth herself a prophetess, to teach and to seduce my servants to commit fornication, and to eat things sacrificed unto idols (Revelation 2:20).

And I gave her space to repent of her fornication; and she repented not (Revelation 2:21).

And the rest of the men which were not killed by these plagues yet repented not of the works of their hands, that they should not worship devils, and idols of gold, and silver, and brass, and stone, and of wood: which neither can see, nor hear, nor walk (Revelation 9:21).

And there followed another angel, saying, Babylon is fallen, is fallen, that great city, because she made all nations drink of the wine of the wrath of her fornication (Revelation 14:8).

With whom the kings of the earth have committed for-nication, and the inhabitants of the earth have been made drunk with the wine of her fornication (Revelation 17:2).

And the woman was arrayed in purple and scarlet color, and decked with gold and precious stones and pearls, having a golden cup in her hand full of abominations and filthiness of her fornication (Revelation 17:4).

For all nations have drunk of the wine of the wrath of her fornication, and the kings of the earth have committed for-nication with her, and the merchants of the earth are waxed rich through the abundance of her delicacies (Revelation 18:3).

And the kings of the earth, who have committed fornica-tion and lived deliciously with her, shall bewail her, and la-ment for her, when they shall see the smoke of her burning (Revelation 18:9).

For true and righteous are his judgments: for he hath judged the great whore, which did corrupt the earth with her fornication, and hath avenged the blood of his servants at her hand (Revelation 19:2).

What? know ye not that he which is joined to an harlot is one body? for two, saith he, shall be one flesh. But he that is joined unto the Lord is one spirit. Flee fornication. Every sin that a man doeth is without the body; but he that committeth fornication sinneth against his own body (1 Corinthians 6:16-18).

Chapter Thirteen

HEALTH FACTS ABOUT STD

According to the CDC, STDs are diseases that are passed from one person to another through sexual contact. These include chlamydia, gonorrhea, genital herpes, human papillomavirus (HPV), syphilis, and HIV. Many of these STDs do not show symptoms for a long time. Even without symptoms, they can still be harmful and passed on during sex.

How are STDs spread?

You can get an STD by having vaginal, anal, or oral sex with someone who has an STD. Anyone who is sexually active can get an STD. You don't even have to "go all the way" (have anal or vaginal sex) to get an STD. This is because some STDs, like herpes and HPV, are spread by skin-to-skin contact.

How common are STDs?

STDs are common, especially among young people. There are about 20 million new cases of STDs each year in the United States. About half of these infections are in

SPIRITUAL SIDE OF SEX

people between the ages of 15 and 24. Young people are at greater risk of getting an STD for several reasons:

- Young women's bodies are biologically more prone to STDs.
- Some young people do not get the recommended STD tests.
- Many young people are hesitant to talk openly and honestly with a doctor or nurse about their sex lives.
- Not having insurance or transportation can make it more difficult for young people to access STD testing.
- Some young people have more than one sex partner.

What can I do to protect myself?

The surest way to protect yourself against STDs is to not have sex. That means not having any vaginal, anal, or oral sex ("abstinence"). There are many things to consider before having sex. It's okay to say "no" if you don't want to have sex.

- If you do decide to have sex, you and your partner should get tested for STDs beforehand. Make sure that you and your partner use a condom from start to finish every time you have oral, anal, or vaginal sex. Know where to get condoms and how to use them correctly. It is not safe to stop using condoms unless you've both been tested for STDs, know your results, and are in a mutually monogamous relationship.
- Mutual monogamy means that you and your partner both agree to only have sexual contact with each other. This can help protect against STDs, as long as you've both been tested and know you're STD-free.

- Before you have sex, talk with your partner about how you will prevent STDs and pregnancy. If you think you're ready to have sex, you need to be ready to protect your body. You should also talk to your partner ahead of time about what you will and will not do sexually. Your partner should always respect your right to say no to anything that doesn't feel right.
- Make sure you get the health care you need. Ask a doctor or nurse about STD testing and about vaccines against HPV and hepatitis B.
- Girls and young women may have extra needs to protect their reproductive health. Talk to your doctor or nurse about regular cervical cancer screening, and chlamydia and gonorrhea testing. You may also want to discuss unintended pregnancy and birth control.
- Avoid mixing alcohol and/or recreational drugs with sex. If you use alcohol and drugs, you are more likely to take risks, like not using a condom or having sex with someone you normally wouldn't have sex with.

If I get an STD, how will I know?

Many STDs don't cause any symptoms that you would notice. The only way to know for sure if you have an STD is to get tested. You can get an STD from having sex with someone who has no symptoms. Just like you, that person might not even know he or she has an STD.

Where can I get tested?

There are places that offer teen-friendly, confidential, and free STD tests. This means that no one has to find out you've been tested. Visit Get Tested to find an STD testing location near you.

Can STDs be treated?

Your doctor can prescribe medicine to cure some STDs, like chlamydia and gonorrhea. Other STDs, like herpes, can't be cured, but you can take medicine to help with the symptoms. If you are ever treated for an STD, be sure to finish all of your medicine, even if you feel better before you finish it all. Ask the doctor or nurse about testing and treatment for your partner, too. You and your partner should avoid having sex until you've both been treated. Otherwise, you may continue to pass the STD back and forth. It is possible to get an STD again (after you've been treated), if you have sex with someone who has an STD.

What happens if I don't treat an STD?

Some curable STDs can be dangerous if they aren't treated. For example, if left untreated, chlamydia and gonorrhea can make it difficult—or even impossible—for a woman to get pregnant. You also increase your chances of getting HIV if you have an untreated STD. Some STDs, like HIV, can be fatal if left untreated.

What if my partner or I have an incurable STD?

Some STDs, like herpes and HIV, aren't curable, but a doctor can prescribe medicine to treat the symptoms.

If you are living with an STD, it's important to tell your partner before you have sex. Although it may be uncomfortable to talk about your STD, open and honest conversation can help your partner make informed decisions to protect his or her health.

If I have questions, who can answer them?

If you have questions, talk to a parent or other trusted adult. Don't be afraid to be open and honest with them about your concerns. If you're ever confused or need advice, they're the first place to start. After all, they were young once, too. Talking about sex with a parent or another adult doesn't need to be a one-time conversation. It's best to leave the door open for conversations in the future. It's also important to talk honestly with a doctor or nurse. Ask which STD tests they recommend for you.

STD information and referrals to STD Clinics
CDC-INFO
1-800-CDC-INFO (800-232-4636)

Different Types of STDs (STIs)
Please Stay safe

- Learn how to avoid STDs (STLs) and what to do if you may have one.
- If you are having sex, talk to your doctor about testing for STDs.
- Learn about National Women and Girls HIV/AIDS Awareness Day.

Sexually transmitted diseases (STDs) are infections that you can get by having sex or skin-to-skin contact between genital with someone who has an STD.

STDs are also sometimes called sexually transmitted infections or STIs. Whatever you call them, they can cause serious health problems. And they happen a lot to young people: About half of all new infections happen to people ages 15 to 24.

There are more than 25 STDs caused by many different bacteria and viruses. Each STD has its own symptoms, but some have similar symptoms. One thing is clear: If you get an unusual discharge, sore, or rash, especially in the public area, you should stop having sex and see a doctor right away.

Check out the symptoms, tests, and treatments for common STDs below.

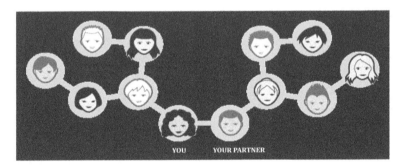

One partner can expose you to many diseases. You are at risk of getting all of the STDs that your partner's past and present partners have had.

Chlamydia

Chlamydia is a very common STD. Women who have chlamydia are much more likely to get HIV if they are exposed to it.

Also, if it's not treated, chlamydia can cause serious problems, like pelvic inflammatory disease and not being able to have a baby.

What are some symptoms?

Because chlamydia often doesn't cause symptoms, experts recommend that teens who have sex get tested for it every year.

Symptoms can include:
- Unusual vaginal discharge (not the clear or slightly white fluid women often have)
- Burning when urinating
- Bleeding between periods
- Pain in your belly area
- Back pain
- Nausea
- Fever
- Pain during sex

How could you get it?

It is passed through vaginal, anal, or oral sex. A mother also can pass it to her baby when the baby goes through her vagina. If you are pregnant, you should get tested for chlamydia.

How do you know if you have it?

A health care provider will test a specimen (a sample of cells) from your vagina or cervix. You might even be able to get the specimen yourself, which is pretty easy.
The provider might test your urine instead.

SPIRITUAL SIDE OF SEX

How is it treated?

Chlamydia can be cured with antibiotics. Any of your sex partners should be treated, too, in case they caught it (and can give it back to you or someone else). Don't have sex until your treatment is finished.

Genital herpes

Genital herpes is caused by a virus called herpes simplex virus (HSV). There are two types of herpes virus that cause genital herpes: HSV-1 and HSV-2. Usually, genital herpes is HSV-2. But a person with HSV-1 — that's oral herpes or cold sores around a person's mouth — can pass the virus to another person's genitals during oral sex.

Genital herpes can increase the risk of HIV infection. That's because HIV can enter the body more easily where there's a break in the skin, such as a herpes sore.

What are some symptoms?

Some people have no symptoms. Symptoms can include:

- Small red bumps, blisters, or open sores in the genital area or anus (bottom) that can hurt a lot
- Fever, headache, and muscle aches
- Swollen glands in the genital area
- Itching or burning in genital area
- Pain in legs, buttocks, or genital area
- Pain when urinating

Symptoms may go away and then come back. Sores usually heal after 2 to 4 weeks. If the sores are mild, a person might think they are just bug bites or other skin problem.
How could you get it?

Herpes can be spread by vaginal, anal, and oral sex or other sexual contact. It spreads most easily through contact with open sores, but you also can catch herpes from skin that doesn't look like it has a sore. Condoms give only limited protection against herpes.

Herpes also can be passed to a baby during birth, which can be very serious.

How do you know if you have it?

Your doctor may be able to see sores and take fluid from them to be sent to a lab for testing. If not, he or she may do a blood test.

How is it treated?

There is no cure, but medicine can help make the times when you have sores shorter and less frequent. Even if you're taking medicine, you can spread herpes when you have sores, so wait until they're gone to have sex. And even if you have no sores, there's still a chance you can pass along the disease. If you have several outbreaks in a year, a daily medicine may lower your chance of spreading herpes.

Gonorrhea

Gonorrhea is a common STD. Recently, it has gotten harder to treat successfully because germs have built up resistance (strength) in fighting the medicine used against them.

Having gonorrhea can make you more likely to get HIV if you're exposed to it. Untreated gonorrhea can cause serious problems, including not being able to get pregnant, even if you don't have symptoms. It can also sometimes spread to the blood, joints, heart, or even the brain.

Any young person who has had sex should be tested for gonorrhea.

What are some symptoms?

Most people have no symptoms or just mild ones. Symptoms can include:

- Yellow or green vaginal discharge that may smell bad
- Pain or burning when urinating (peeing)
- Pain during sex
- Vaginal bleeding between menstrual periods

Gonorrhea infection can also be in your throat, which may cause a sore throat. It can also spread to your eyes, causing symptoms like pain and sensitivity to light.

It can also be in your anus (bottom). Symptoms there include:

- Anal discharge
- Anal itching
- Soreness
- Bleeding
- Painful bowel movements

How could you get it?

You can get gonorrhea during vaginal, oral, or anal sex with someone who has it. It also can be passed to a baby when the baby goes through your vagina during birth and can cause serious problems for the baby.

How do you know if you have it?

Your doctor will do a urine test or take a specimen (a small sample of cells, such as from your cervix or vagina to test.

How is it treated?

Gonorrhea can be cured with antibiotics, but some cases can be harder to treat. Any partners need to be treated, too, or you can pass the infection back and forth. Don't have sex until you and any partners finish treatment.

Hepatitis B

Hepatitis B is caused by a virus that attacks the liver. It's also called HBV. If hepatitis B doesn't go away, it can lead to liver cancer and other serious liver problems.

Most babies now get vaccinated for HBV. Talk to your doctor or look at your health records to see if you were vaccinated. If not, you should get the shots now to help prevent this serious illness.

What are some symptoms?

You may have no symptoms, or you may have some, including:

- Yellow skin or yellowing of the whites of the eyes
- Tiredness
- Dark-colored urine
- Stomach pain
- Loss of appetite
- Nausea and vomiting
- Diarrhea
- Low fever
- Headache or muscle aches
- Hives or skin rash
- Joint pain and swelling

Symptoms usually appear about 6 to 12 weeks after you get infected.

How could you get it?

You can get hepatitis B when an infected person's blood, semen, or other bodily fluid enters your body. This can happen during sex. It can also happen if you:

- Share drug needles with an infected person
- Get a tattoo or piercing using a needle with the virus on it
- Use an infected person's toothbrush or razor

A baby also can get hepatitis B from its mother during birth. If you are pregnant, get tested. See below for other reasons a person may need to be tested.

How do you know if you have it?

A blood test determines if you have it. If you are pregnant, you need to be tested. People who face a higher risk of possibly getting hepatitis B also should get tested. Ask your doctor about testing if:

- You were born in a country where hepatitis B is common (such as countries in Africa and Asia)
- You were born in the United States but one of your parents was born in a country where hepatitis B is common and you did not get a hepatitis B vaccine as a baby
- You live with someone who has hepatitis B
- You have other risks for hepatitis B, like using injection drugs, having HIV, or having sex with someone who has hepatitis B

You can learn more about hepatitis B.

How is it treated?

There is no cure for hepatitis B. Often, it goes away without treatment, but some young people can develop life-long problems from it. Hepatitis B may be treated with certain medicines that can help slow down the infection. These medicines are not safe for pregnant women.
I
f you have recently been exposed to the hepatitis B virus, see a doctor right away. You may be able to get treatment to lower the risk of coming down with the disease.

HIV/AIDS

Human immunodeficiency virus, or HIV, is the virus that can cause AIDS (acquired immunodeficiency syndrome). HIV and AIDS weaken the body's ability to fight infections and diseases. Learn more about HIV/AIDS.

What are some symptoms?

Women and girls with HIV may have no symptoms for years. Even if HIV causes no symptoms, it is still causing problems with your body's immune system that need treatment as early as possible. HIV can lead to AIDS.

Some people have flu-like symptoms within the first few weeks or months after they get infected with HIV.

Some people have flu-like symptoms within the first few weeks or months after they get infected with HIV.

Symptoms of AIDS include:

- Weight loss
- Fevers, chills, and night sweats
- Being very tired
- Headache
- Diarrhea, vomiting, and nausea
- Mouth, genital, or anal sores
- Dry cough
- Rash
- Swollen lymph nodes
- Other STDs (STIs), vaginal yeast infections, and other vaginal infections
- Pelvic inflammatory disease (PID) that does not get better with treatment
- Menstrual cycle changes, like not having periods or having heavy bleeding
- Human papillomavirus (HPV) infections, which can cause genital warts and cervical cancer

You cannot rely on symptoms to know whether you have HIV. More than half of young people with HIV don't know they have it.

You have to get tested to know if you have HIV.

Get tested at least once if:

- You are 15 or older
- You are younger than 15 but do things that put you at an increased risk of HIV, such as having unprotected sex or having sex with someone who uses injection drugs
- You are pregnant

Your doctor may suggest that you get tested more than once if you do things that increase your risk of HIV, such as have unprotected sex or use injection drugs. Find a place to get tested.

How could you get it?

You can get infected with HIV when blood, semen (cum), pre-semen (pre-cum), vaginal fluid, anal mucus (fluids in your anus), or breast milk from an infected person enters your body. This can happen during oral, anal, or vaginal sex. It also can happen when these fluids get into an open wound or sore. You also can get HIV from sharing needles for drugs, tattoos, or piercings with an infected person.

Babies can get HIV during pregnancy, birth, and breastfeeding. Treatments can lower the risk during pregnancy and birth, but mothers with HIV should not breastfeed.

You can't get HIV from casual contact, like sneezing or touching.

How do you know if you have it?

HIV tests use blood, oral fluids, or urine. You can ask your doctor or a health clinic about testing. Only two home tests are approved by the FDA: Home Access Express HIV-1 Test System and OraQuick In-Home HIV Test. Be careful: You can buy other HIV home tests online, but they are not approved by the FDA and may give wrong results.

How is it treated?

There is no cure for HIV, but there are treatments that help infected people live longer and healthier lives. It's important to get treatment early.

Human papillomavirus (HPV)

Human papillomavirus, or HPV, is the most common STD in the United States. In fact, most people who have sex get it at some point in their lives.

HPV often goes away on its own. But some types of HPV can cause genital warts, cervical cancer, and other types of cancer.

The HPV vaccine can help prevent the types of HPV that cause most cases of cervical cancer and genital warts. Ask your parents or doctor about getting vaccinated. Keep in mind that the vaccine works much better if you get it before you ever have sex.

What are some symptoms?

Some people have no symptoms. Symptoms can include:

- Warts on the genitals or inner thighs or around the anus (bottom). These can be flat or raised and alone or in groups. They may cause itching, burning, or pain.
- Growths on the cervix and vagina that the person often can't see

HPV can be passed to a partner even if the infected person has no symptoms.

How could you get it?

Most often, HPV is passed during vaginal or anal sex. You can also get it through oral sex or through contact between your genitals and the genitals of someone with HPV.

How do you know if you have it?

Your doctor may look at the genital area to check for warts. A Pap test can find cervical cell changes early, so they can be treated before they turn into cancer.

How is it treated?

There is no treatment for HPV, but there are treatments for the conditions that it can cause, like genital warts and cervical cell changes. For example, warts can be removed through special medications or through minor surgery.

Pubic lice

Lice (a kind of tiny insect) that feed on human blood. Also known as "crabs."

What are some symptoms?

Symptoms can include:

- Itching in the public area
- Finding lice or eggs attached to your pubic hair
- Sores from bites or scratching
- Rust-colored spots on your underwear
- Mild fever and tiredness if you've been bitten by a large number of lice

How could you get it?

Usually a person gets it through skin-to-skin contact with someone who already has it. It's also possible to get it from things like towels, sheets, and clothes.

How do you know if you have it?

You may be able to see the lice yourself, but a doctor can tell you if you have them. If you have lice, the doctor should check you for other STDs.

How is it treated?

A prescription or over-the-counter medicine can kill the adult lice and egg lice. You should also wash any sheets and clothes that could have lice in them, using hot water. You should avoid sexual contact until your treatment is finished.

Syphilis

Syphilis that is not treated can lead to serious problems and even death. Also, the sores caused by syphilis make it easier to get or give someone HIV during sex.

What are some symptoms?

An infected person may not have any symptoms for years, but he or she can still give the disease to someone else. Different stages have different symptoms.

Symptoms in the first (primary) stage appear 10 to 90 days after getting infected. They include:

- A painless sore, usually in the genital area, but possibly on the lips or other parts of the body that had contact with a syphilis sore from another person.
- Swollen lymph glands

Sores heal on their own in around 3 to 6 weeks. But if the infection is not treated, a secondary stage follows.

Symptoms of that stage include:

- Rash on the palms and soles of the feet that usually doesn't itch and goes away on its own
- Fever
- Swollen lymph glands and sore throat
- Patchy hair loss
- Raised gray, warty-looking areas in moist places, such as your genital area, armpits, and anus (bottom)
- Headaches and muscle aches

- Weight loss
- Tiredness

If the infection is still not treated, it moves on to a hidden (latent) stage. Then it can possibly enter a last stage. During this stage there can be damage to the brain, nerves, eyes, heart, and blood vessels. Some people may even die.

How could you get it?

You can get syphilis through direct contact with a syphilis sore. Sores usually are on the genitals, vagina, or anus (bottom). Sores also can be on the lips and in the mouth. That means you can get it during vaginal, anal, or oral sex but also by touching a sore with an open cut you have.

A pregnant woman also can pass syphilis to the baby she is carrying, which can be very dangerous. If you are pregnant, get tested.

How do you know if you have it?

A health care professional can do a blood test or take a sample from a sore to learn if you have syphilis.

How is it treated?

If it is treated early, syphilis can be cured with antibiotics.

Trichomoniasis

Trichomoniasis is caused by a parasite (a tiny organism that feeds off you). It is sometimes called "trich." Trichomoniasis is very common in sexually active young women. Having trichomoniasis increases your chances of getting HIV if you're exposed to it.

What are some symptoms?

Some women don't have symptoms, but those who do can have symptoms appear between 5 and 28 days after getting infected. Symptoms can include:

- Foamy, yellow-green vaginal discharge with a strong odor
- Discomfort during sex and when urinating
- Irritation and itching of the genital area
- Sometimes, lower abdominal pain

How could you get it?

You can get trichomoniasis from vaginal sex or skin-to-skin genital contact.

How do you know if you have it?

Your health care provider will likely give you a pelvic exam and take a sample of your vaginal fluid to test. If you have trichomoniasis, your doctor should check you for other STDs.

How is it treated?

Trichomoniasis usually can be cured with antibiotics. Your partner should be treated, too. You should not have sex until the treatment is finished and you both have no symptoms.

Compilation from Girlshealth.org

Things I want You to Know as We Pray Now

It would be a mistake to close this important material without showing you strategic application of how to begin the practical aspect of achieving your freedom. I want to engage in important prayers with you by outlining different prayer points, so you could follow the directions. You may have to add more prayer points or include other areas as you go depending on your personal issues. Jesus said, my Father worketh, hitherto I work!

In every process of deliverance, understanding how to begin is the key to seeing yourself free from demonic powers. You will not only be healthy — spiritually and physically but also free from demonic pollution and de-filement. In many parts of the world there are not enough knowledge of deliverance so you may not have anyone to readily help you. Sometimes, you may experience differ-ent attacks in your sleep and your Church base may not know how to assist you. I want you to stand firmly and know that no devil has the right to dwell in your body. You must find time to begin the process of self-deliverance. Our environment and atmosphere are full of evil spirits and unless you allow the LORD to cleanse and keep your life pure, devils will rush all over your life.

Demons are fallen angels: they are spirit beings, which is to say that they are like breath or air. They are incor-poreal and during deliverance they escape through the breathing passage including any other orifice. It is the rea-son why some people may emit foul odors or pass gas. During deliverance sessions we may ask people to remain silent and sometimes, we may ask them to breath in and out periodically. For demons to go out, they need passage ways or open doors of exit, just as they enter through entrance gates. The many ways demons come out of people includes but not limited to convulsing, breathing, yawning, choking, crying, sweating, vomiting, falling and rolling on the floor, screaming, etc. Demonic manifestations vary and often, they represent the exhibitions of behavioral patterns. You must know that you are dealing with real personalities. The stages of deliverance involve certain demons leaving much quicker but those who are deeply rooted and entrenched in people's lives takes more time and diligent effort to cast out. There also stubbornly reluctant demons that must take the help or assistance of other people of God to dislodge. Even if you are dealing with highly strong powers, you must persist until they come out. This may take some time so always remember! When different powers are ganged up to create a problem, you may not see total breakthrough until they are all driven away. The victim will continue to experience levels of progress and improvements as more and more territories are liberated. Always, legal grounds are points of contest and resistance until the legal holds are seized from all occupying powers.

Let us look at some of the stages of engaging in self-deliverance:

Because deliverance is part of spiritual warfare, you may begin with praise and worship and then, gather together Scriptures that promise deliverance and speak out these words. Such Scriptures are:

Surely he shall deliver thee from the snare of the fowler, and from the noisome pestilence (Psalms 91:3).

And the God of peace shall bruise Satan under your feet shortly. The grace of our Lord Jesus Christ be with you. Amen (Romans 16:20).

Christ hath redeemed us from the curse of the law, being made a curse for us: for it is written, Cursed is every one that hangeth on a tree: *That the blessing of Abraham might come on the Gentiles through Jesus Christ; that we might receive the promise of the Spirit through faith* (Galatians 3:13-14).

In whom we have redemption through his blood, the forgiveness of sins, according to the riches of his grace (Ephesians 1:7).

Blotting out the handwriting of ordinances that was against us, which was contrary to us, and took it out of the way, nailing it to his cross; And having spoiled principalities and powers, he made a shew of them openly, triumphing over them in it (Colossians 2:14-15).

And the Lord shall deliver me from every evil work, and will preserve me unto his heavenly kingdom: to whom be glory for ever and ever. Amen (2 Timothy 4:18).

And they overcame him by the blood of the Lamb, and by the word of their testimony; and they loved not their lives unto the death (Revelation 12:11).

Now, break all covenants and initiations, cut off all links, detach yourself from all attachments, disassociate from all associations and destroy all known and unknown altars. Break all curses and take authority over all spirits that are connected to your life through these avenues. Go through your family line and trace the bloodline to remove yourself from all evil inheritances. In the Bible, all idol and satanic altars were destroyed and the altar of the LORD was raised up and rebuilt to offer sacrifices unto the LORD. This is where you invoke or engage the redemptive blood of Jesus Christ — the Lamb of God. Ask the Holy Spirit to appropriate the blood of Jesus upon your spirit, soul and body. Relief all evil priests and priestesses from their duties and terminate their assignments and cut off all demonic contracts with them, etc.

Begin to call out every part of your life — all the organs in your body out of the hands and prisons of the enemy. Even if you begin to experience demonic manifestation, you do not have to be afraid. Exercise diligence and maintain your focus on driving the spirits out. Command every spirit that is not of the Living God to immediately depart in Jesus name. You are firmly demanding with authority that they vacate the premises and quarters of your life without further delay. Remind the spirits that they can no longer hide anywhere in your body. Let them know you are aware of what they are doing and they must stop. Engage them directly and speak clearly — giving them what direction to follow. Take a brief pause or moment of silence to allow for them to begin to exist from your body. Breathe in and out occasionally so they will follow your breath and leave. Maintain the process until the end of every session. Ask the Holy Spirit to fill and occupy every place they vacated from your body. Ask the LORD God to surround you with His defense and to place angels around you.

For God is the King of all the earth: sing ye praises with understanding (Psalms 47:7).

And the LORD will create upon every dwelling place of mount Zion, and upon her assemblies, a cloud and smoke by day, and the shining of a flaming fire by night: for upon all the glory shall be a defence (Isaiah 4:5).

For I, saith the LORD, will be unto her a wall of fire round about, and will be the glory in the midst of her (Zechariah 2:5).

And they overcame him by the blood of the Lamb, and by the word of their testimony; and they loved not their lives unto the death (Revelation 12:11).

Deliverance takes process and the stages of progression differ significantly. Sometimes, it is because of many factors:

1. How long the spirit may have been in a person's life.
2. The powers and fortifications that the spirits have built inside the individuals.
3. The levels and measures of the power of God working in the lives of those administering deliverance.
4. The willful determination of the individuals seeking after deliverance.
5. The depth of the knowledge of the Word of God.
6. The detest or utter hatred of sin.

To be effective in self-deliverance, you must be very determined as well as disciplined. A stronghold takes strong support to tear it down and likewise, soft targets are easier to defeat. Strong bondage takes strong power to challenge and often, you may underestimate the severity of your situation until you begin to dig deeper for your freedom. Demons use small open-doors to create giant open gates; therefore, a foothold may lead to a stronghold and taking back your freedom may take great effort.

Pray: In the name of Jesus Christ, I denounce and renounce spirit husband and spirit wife, spirit boyfriend and girlfriend and all astral projected souls cleaving to my soul and body.

I separate and divorce myself from all spiritual marriages by the blood of Jesus. I serve all spirit husband, wife, boyfriend and girlfriend with the bill of divorcement now in Jesus name.

I break all spiritual marriage vows, oaths, allegiances, ceremonies and consents. I demand for a total release of every part of me now.

Every proprietary belongings, items, objects and material embedded or deposited in my body catch fire and burn to ashes in Jesus name. I command all evil marriage tokens to turn to dust.

Every power operating or functioning against my physical marriage life cease and decease.

I break all marriage covenants, agreements, submission and subjection to spirit husband, spirit wife, spirit boyfriend and girlfriend in Jesus name.

I command the fire of God to burn to nothing all marriage garments, rings, pictures, and other records or certificate of marriage.

I cut off all blood covenants, soul-ties, sex-ties and demonic ties. I disown and I reject all spiritual offspring conceived and born to the marriage in Jesus name.

I withdraw my blood, secretion, body fluid, sperm or any other part of my life dedicated, committed or sacrificed on the altar of the spirit husband, spirit wife, spirit boyfriend and spirit girlfriend.

I overturn every plan or scheme of the enemy to destabilize and sabotage my life in Jesus name.

Evil powers assigned to defile and pollute my spirit, soul and body, catch fire and burn to ashes now.

I release thunder and lightning against all sodomizing and rapist powers: I command darkness and blindness to arrest them in Jesus name.

I bring death and destruction upon all evil spirit children in my life.

I bind every spirit husband, wife, boyfriend and girlfriend tormenting my life and my marriage: I command you to lose your hold now and depart from me in Jesus name.

I return back all properties belonging to spirit husband, wife, boyfriend and girlfriend including all dowry and everything used for the marriage wedding.

I command the blood of Jesus Christ to purge my body from all sexual deposits, sexual transmitted disease, sickness and sexual transmitted demons. I call for the fire of

God to consume all roots and burn up all unclean things released into my life.

I cut off the head of the serpent released into my body and I dry up all the venom injected to cause me harm. I command all material deposits inside my womb to be vomited out now.

Father, I pray that you would heal all damages, hurts, wounds and injuries inflicted upon any part of my body and restore my earthly marriage in Jesus name.

I cancel all evil pronouncements, curses, spells, hexes, linx, incantations, enchantments or other bewitchment placed upon my life and marriage in Jesus name.

I denounce, renounce and reject all names and nicknames or titles and positions given to me by spirit husband, wife, boyfriend and girlfriend.

I turn my back now and I command spirit husband, wife, boyfriend and girlfriend to turn their backs on me in Jesus name.

I declare openly that Jesus Christ is my Savior, LORD and Husband forever. I declare before Heaven and Earth that I am married to Jesus Christ.

I soak my life in the blood of the Lamb and I delete and erase all satanic marks placed on my life. I declare that I am crucified with Christ, buried and resurrected with Him and seated at the right hand of the Father. I destroy all satanic images and I diffuse myself from infusion of the satanic nature. I declare that I am in the image of God after His likeness through Jesus Christ.

I release myself from the strongholds and bondage of spirit husband, wife, boyfriend and girlfriend in Jesus name.

I destroy all manipulation and controlling devices used to antagonize and destabilize my physical marriage and family.

I command all copyrights, trademarks, service marks, archives and databases retaining any and all copies, duplicates, replica or false images of my wedding, marriage certificate and ceremonial vows in Jesus name.

I command anything written in the cycle of the moon against my life and everything programmed into the sun, moon and the star including those in my gene and DNA to be dismantled, blotted out and destroyed.

I command all evil writings or engravings against me to erased and destroyed now and I object to consent to incriminating evidences against me. And I repent of all sins, trespasses, iniquities and transgressions before the LORD.

I legislate against all spirits that are unwilling to leave and by the blood of Jesus Christ I ask that all evidences be removed and for injunctions to be signed judicially to remove them from my life.

I file for counterclaims against all evil marriage reports and ask for all demonic exhibitions and testimonies against me to be vacated, dismissed and destroyed in Jesus name.

I close all doors, gates and avenues of life and my house against the spirit husband, wife, boyfriend and girlfriend now.

I command utter destruction upon the palaces of the River gods and goddesses, queen of the Coast, marine Kingdom, queen of heaven and the agents and agencies representing their interests to be consumed by the fire of judgment in Jesus name.

I legislate against all wicked laws against my life, and I command the seasons and times to reverse the schedules, calendars and orders of events now.

I withdraw myself from the altars of the god and deities that rule over the world and over the land. I command the altars to break up to pieces. Every altar speaking against me and every tongue risen against me in judgment be condemned in Jesus name.

Every nation or Kingdom raised up to hinder or stop the purpose of a God for my life and my destiny fail from your foundation.

I command every veil covering my life, every wall of partition and all fortifications causing me stagnation to break from the ground.

I call for the fire of God to destroy all satanic seed in my womb. I cut off all access to my reproductive gates and I disconnect myself from all parental transferred spirits attached to my umbilical passage in Jesus name.

I cripple all forms of witchcraft manifestations and forms.

I command all spirits of oppression to come out now.

I cut off all sexual blood covenants.

I break all sexual soul-ties emanating from previous relationships.

I destroy all sexual curses and bondage in Jesus name.

Author's Note of Thanks

Prophet Dan Effiong, Dallas , Texas, USA.

Pastor Christian and Robin Harfouche, Pensacola, Florida. USA.

Apostle Charles and Donna Ndifon, Rhode Island, USA.

Apostle Paul Eneche, Dunamis International, Abuja, Nigeria, West Africa.

Apostle Victor Bessong, Netword International, USA.

Prophet Gideon Kabila, Zambia, Africa.

And many other precious men and women of God around the nation and around the world.

BIBLIOGRAPHY

Hill King, John. Spies Among the Church, Harvesters Publisher, NY: Harvesters Books. 2015.

Brown, Rebecca. Becoming a Vessel of Honor. Woodburn, OR: Fortress Books. 1992.

He Came to Set the Captives Free. New Kensington, PA: Whitaker House, 1997.

Prepare for War. New Kensington, PA: Whitaker House, 1997.

Unbroken Curses. Springdale, PA: Whitaker House, 1995.

Brown, Stephen W. Follow the Wind. Grand Rapids, MI: Baker Books, 1999. Buckingham, Jamie. Daughter of Destiny: Kathryn Kuhlman, Her Story. Plainfield, NJ: Logos International, 1976.

Cerullo, Morris. The Last Great Anointing. Ventura, CA: Renew, 1999. Chambers, Oswald. My Utmost for His Highest. New York, NY: Dodd, Mead & Company, 1935.

Cymbala, Jim. Fresh Wind, Fresh Fire. Grand Rapids, MI: Zondervan, 2003. Dawson, Joy. Intercession, Thrilling and Fulfilling. Seattle, WA: YWAM Publishers, 1997.

Intimate Friendship With God. Old Tappan, NJ: Chosen Books, 1986.

Dollar, Creflo A. Understanding God's Purpose for the Anointing. New York, NY: Creflo Dollar Ministries, 1992.

Uprooting the Spirit of Fear. Tulsa, OK: Harrison House, 2002.

Fenelon, Francois. Fenelon: Meditations on the Heart of God. Brewster, MA: Paraclete Press, 1997.

Talking With God. Brewster, MA: Paraclete Press, 1997.

The Royal Way of the Cross. Orleans, MA: Paraclete Press, 1982.

Finney, Charles G. God's Call. New Kensington, PA: Whitaker House, 1999.

Power From on High. Springdale, PA: Whitaker House, 1996.

The Secret of Faith. New Kensington, PA: Whitaker House, 1999.

Guyon, Madame. Experiencing God Through Prayer. Springdale, PA: Whitaker House, 1984.

Union With God. Sargent, GA: The Seed Sowers, 1981.

Hagin, Kenneth E. Healing Forever Settled. Tulsa, OK: K. Hagin Ministries, 1989.

Plans, Purposes, & Pursuits. Tulsa, OK: Faith Library Publications, 1988.

The Believer's Authority. Tulsa, OK: Faith Library Publications, 1984. Hammond, Frank, and Ida Mae Hammond. Pigs in the Parlor. Kirkwood, MO: Impact Books, 1973.

Hammond, Frank D. Our Warfare: Against Demons & Territorial Spirits. Kirkwood, MO: Impact Books, 1991, 1994.

Demons and Deliverance in the Ministry of Jesus. Kirkwood, MO: Impact Books, 1991.

ABOUT THE AUTHOR

Prophetess Dr. Evette Young was born and raised in New Orleans, Louisiana. She is a license and ordained Minister of the Gospel of Jesus Christ. She is the daughter of Mr. and Mrs. Emanuel and Evelyn Young. The wife of Dr. John K. Hill, and Mother of Anointed Evelyn Divine. She is an upcoming and a New Strong voice in the Kingdom of God. The power of God is extremely evident in her life and Ministry. Countless lives have been changed and transformed through her work. Dr. Evette is a prolific preacher who is empowered to release the fire of God. God has truly placed on her life the prophetic mantle, the working of the miraculous, healing, teaching and preaching. She has an incredible deliverance power of God on her life to free people from addictions, sexual perversions, abusive relationships, all forms of demonic bondage, and satanic works, etc. There are numerous testimonies and praise reports of bodies being healed and set free in her ministry. Dr. Evette is a tremendous, dynamic Woman of Prayer. She has impeccable integrity, and live a holy life unto the Lord. She is dedicated and committed to her God-given ministry assignment for the Kingdom of God. She has the Spirit of Excellence. She is a woman of class, servitude, and with uncanny boldness, she powerfully declares the unadulterated Gospel of Jesus Christ. Dr. Evette is a Graduate of World Harvest Bible

College, where the Honorable Rod Parsley is founder and Pastor, and Graduate of International Miracle Institute, where Apostle Christian and Robin Harfouche are the Founders. She holds an A A, MA, MA, PhD in theology y. She has appeared on WACTV Live, and World TV Network and other Christian Networks.

One of her goals is to rescue the little ones who are trapped in the sex trafficking industry. Part of her vision is to open a caring home to nurture and raise them in the love of our Heavenly Father and release them into their Kingdom Destiny! Dr. Evette teaches from the Kingdom perspective - on our Delegated Authority as citizens of Heaven. One of her mandates is to awaken the appetite for the Glory of God within the hearts of the people of God. She teaches primarily on operating as Kings and Priests, functioning in Dominion to subdue the earth and rule over it. Dr. Evette spends her life helping the discouraged, the disenfranchised, and those who have been emotionally wounded, abused, rejected and bound

by all kinds of bondage. Her drive is to empower God's people and help them discover their purposes and reach their full potential and experience true success in every area of their lives! Dr. Evette travels around the nation and the world, declaring the message of the gospel of Jesus Christ with power. Her motivation is to challenge the people of God everywhere to reach for the higher dimensions in their walk with Christ.

Our ministry is passionately built to help others triumph through personal coaching, counseling, mentorship training, seminars and workshops. God's Royal Women Miracle Ministries is focused on helping women know who they are, by helping them learn how to value their unique contribution as women of class, honor and dignity. Many women across the world are absolutely clueless about who they are in Christ. Some are struggling with identity crisis.

Our endeavor is to bring spiritual insight and guide them with wisdom to maximize their full potential in Christ. Dr. Evette courageously pours her life out to help shape the lives of the downcast, bruised, wounded, and scared women using her own life's traumatic experiences. Her desire is to help women learn how to avoid the mistakes and the pitfalls that she walked through herself. Her message is purposed to bring deliverance and total healing and transform lives through the working power of Jesus Christ. Dr. Evette has a conviction to inspire other women to achieve true ladylikeness, which is in Christlikeness. Many women embark upon a search for the "real me" only to be deceived or frustrated in an attempt to become whatever is the present–day image of a woman. True womanhood can never be measured by a man's affections or society praises, but by a woman's own character as defined and esteemed or appreciated by the word of God.

There is no other standard for a true woman of God! And there is no reason why you cannot become all that God has called and ordained you to be in life. At God's Royal Women Ministries, we are a people of ministry. We know that ministry is finding the needs of the people and meeting them according to God's provision and supplies. We are working on building transitional housing for abused women and teenagers, and we are committed to clothing and distributing food to the less privileged or fortunate. The Bible said, by this my Father is glorified that you bear much fruit and so prove to be my disciples (John 15:8). We are laborers in the Kingdom of God, effecting change in our nation and beyond! Our goal is to bring tremendous healing and whole prosperity to spiritually and physically thirsty and hungry women. God's Royal Women Ministries and Dr. Evette will help you discover new strength to accelerate change in your quality of

living, reforming dignity, reputation and respect for all women. We will show you how to overcome challenges and degree of difficulties of life, and how to rise above them all!

CONTACT THE AUTHOR

For more information about:

Prophetess (Dr.) Evette Young- Hill or to contact the author for worldwide speaking engagements

Visit:

Website: www.godsroyalwomen.org

Email: info@godsroyalwomen.org.

Facebook: facebook.com/EvetteYoung.

Youtube: youtube.com/EvetteYoung.

Twitter: twitter.com/EvetteYoung

Additional copies of this book and other book titles from

ROYAL PUBLISHERS™ are available at your local

Bookstore.

To view our catalogue online, visit us at:

www.godsroyalwomen.org

Send a request or contact us:

GOD'S ROYAL WOMEN

A Division of God's Royal Women Solution For Life, Inc.

Phone: 1.504.644.4407

media@godsroyalwomen.org

"Daughters of the Royal Kingdom."

Books by Dr. Evette Yoing

Spiritual Warfare Strategies

Dynamic Power of Prayer

In My Name They Shall Cast Out Evil Spirits

Sex, Reason to Wait

Ultimate Prayer Handbook

Available from your local bookstore or

wv ' ')rg

GOD'S ROYAL WOMEN

A Division of God's Royal Women Solution For Life, Inc.

Give a Gift of True Freedom

We are always looking to reach every household—around the nation and around the world with the message of the love and power of God through Jesus Christ, whether it relates to salvation, healing, deliverance, prosperity or family!

Join us and be a part.

The Lord gave the word: great was the company of those that published it (Psalms 68:11).

As you share the experience in this book, share it also with someone dear to your heart or even a stranger. Give it as a love gift to as many people as you can, and help us reach millions with the love and power of God!

Use Code: SSOS20

For Special Discounted Offer!

Email: offer@godsroyalwomen.org

DR. EVETTE YOUNG

Lightning Source UK Ltd.
Milton Keynes UK
UKHW051253231122
412711UK00012B/375

9 781087 910567